GREECE: THE LEGACY

ESSAYS ON THE HISTORY OF GREECE, ANCIENT, BYZANTINE, AND MODERN

edited by
John A. Koumoulides

University Press of Maryland

Koumoulides, John T. A., 1938-   .
    Greece: the legacy : essays on the history of Greece,
ancient, Byzantine, and modern / edited by John A.
Koumoulides.
        p.   cm.
    Includes bibliographical references and index.
    ISBN 1-883053-43-9
    1. Greece—Civilization—Influence. 2. Greece—
Civilization—Foreign influences. 3. National characteristics,
Greek. 4. Greece—Civilization—20th century—Classical
influences. I. Title.
DF741.K855   1998
949.5—dc21   98-33506
                                                                      CIP

To
Michael and Mary Jaharis

. . . . But Greece and her foundations are
Built below the tide of war
Based on the crystalline sea
Of thought and its eternity.
Her citizens, imperial spirits,
Rule the present from the past . . . .

The world's great age begins anew,
The golden years return,
The earth doth like a snake renew
Her winter weeds outworn . . . .

A brighter Hellas rears its mountains
From waves serener far;
A new Peneus rolls his fountains
Against the morning star . . . .

Another Athens shall arise . . . .

Percy Bysshe Shelley, HELLAS

CONTENTS

v

PREFACE

The Legacy of Greece, edited by the late Sir Richard Livingstone, Fellow
and President of Corpus Christi College, Oxford from 1933 to 1950, was
published in 1921. In the preface of the volume Sir Richard wrote:

> In spite of many differences, no age has had closer affinities with Ancient
> Greece than our own; none has based its deeper life so largely on ideals
> which the Greeks brought into the world. History does not repeat itself.
> Yet, if the twentieth century searched through the past for its nearest
> spiritual kin, it is in the fifth and following centuries before Christ that
> they would be found. Again and again, as we study Greek thought and
> literature, behind the veil woven by time and distance, the face that
> meets us is our own, younger, with fewer lines and wrinkles on its
> features and with more definite and deliberate purpose in its eyes. For
> these reasons we are to-day in a position, as no other age has been, to
> understand Ancient Greece, to learn the lessons it teaches, and, in study-
> ing the ideals and fortunes of men with whom we have so much in
> common, to gain a fuller power of understanding and estimating our
> own. This book—the first of its kind in English—aims at giving some idea
> of what the world owes Greece in various realms of the spirit and the
> intellect, and of what it can still learn from her.[1]

Sir Richard and his ten distinguished colleagues took *Legacy* "in its root-
sense, field by field, beginning with religion and philosophy and ending
with art and architecture." *The Legacy of Greece: A New Appraisal*,
edited by the late Sir Moses Finley, Professor of Ancient History in the
University of Cambridge from 1976 to 1982, and Master of Darwin College,
Cambridge from 1976 to 1982, was published in 1984. Sir Moses, in
describing the difference between his *Legacy* and Sir Richard's *Legacy*,
wrote: "This volume retains that element, on a much reduced scale, and
then proceeds, in each chapter, to examine what later ages, down to our
own, have made of the inheritance from the Greeks. Schematically, one
could say that whereas the original *Legacy* was about Greek culture, this
version is about its meaning in the history of European culture."[2] A third

Legacy: The Greeks and Their Legacy, edited by Sir Kenneth Dover, Professor of Greek at the University of St. Andrews from 1955 to 1976, and President of Corpus Christi College, Oxford from 1976 to 1986, was published in 1988. In 1987 Sir Kenneth published *Greek and the Greeks*, which contained his articles on Greek language and Greek poetry. *The Greeks and Their Legacy* brings together Sir Kenneth's articles on "Greek prose literature and history, the transmission of Greek texts in the Middle Ages, and the part that study of the Greeks has played in our own culture."[3] All three books on the legacy of Ancient Greek civilization and culture are still deservedly very popular.

The continuity of Greek history and culture was presented in *The Greeks and Their Heritages* published in 1981. The book was completed shortly before Arnold Toynbee's death in 1974. *The Greeks and Their Heritages* is a study of the history of Greece from ancient times to the present. In his last great work Professor Toynbee, conscious of "historical details and academic concerns," convincingly examines the forces present in the vitality and continuity of Greek civilization—ancient, Byzantine, and modern. Professor Toynbee states:

> Greek history of periods earlier than the year 338 B.C. is certainly inter-esting and instructive, but so too is Greek history from 338 B.C. onwards down to the present. The post-Hellenic Greeks have no need to be over-awed by their ancestors' achievements in the Hellenic phase of Greek history. The Byzantine Greeks' achievements in architecture and in visual art are likewise both distinctive and great. The Modern Greeks have not only produced great poets; in their war of independence and in their recent resistance-movements to foreign invaders, they have performed feats of heroism that are as fine as their ancestors' feats at Marathon and at Thermopylae, while on a more mundane plane, they have played a highly successful part in the Modern World's commercial life.[4]

In 1987 I edited *Greek Connections: Essays on Culture and Diplo-macy*.[5] The contributors to *Greek Connections* provided in their essays a scholarly perspective to our knowledge of Greece and powerfully illus-trated the impact of Greece beyond its geographic frontiers. Greek history and institutions have long been the admiration and inspiration to other cultures and societies across the continents.

During the academic year 1996–97 a diverse group of scholars visited Ball State University under the auspices of the University's Greek Studies Program. The theme of our 1996–97 lecture series was *The Heritage of Greece: Ancient, Byzantine, and Modern*. The purpose of the lecture series was twofold: first, to strengthen our understanding and appreciation of the classical era; and, second, to help us develop an appreciation of the contributions of Greece and the people of Greece in this century. The present volume contains the papers delivered during the academic year 1996–97, as well as papers delivered at Ball State University, under the aegis of the University's Greek Studies Program, in previous years. The papers of Professor Jasper Griffin, Professor Mary R. Lefkowitz, and Professor Mark Mazower were delivered in 1996–97. The papers of the late Fr. Dr. Joseph Gill, S.M. and the late Professor Sir Ronald Syme, O.M., as well as the essays of Professor Bernard M.W. Knox, Professor Donald M. Nicol, Sir Edward Peck, and Sir David Hunt, and the essay by the editor, were read at Ball State University in previous years. They are included in the present volume because of their historical importance and relevance to the 1996–97 theme.

The ten chapters that comprise this book have been organized into four parts. The first part deals with the ancient world. The second part deals with the Byzantine era. The transition period is presented in the third section. The fourth part presents critical episodes in the world of Greece during the twentieth century as well as the importance of the Greek diaspora in the history of Greece. "The Greeks, like the Jews and the Armenians, are pre-eminently a people of the diaspora or 'dispersion', scattered in communities great and small in many parts of the world."[6]

Greece: The Legacy is not a history of Greece, but an attempt to share with the greater public the scholarship of distinguished individuals who, under the auspices of the Greek Studies program, visited Ball State University and delivered lectures on various aspects of the history and culture of Greece, its continuity, and its contributions to western history and civilization.

Greece: The Legacy is intended for students of Greece, both professional and amateur. The book embraces a wide span of Greek history and culture. The authors in their papers reflect the most scholarly and respected thought in their fields. I hope that *Greece: The Legacy* will not only be rewarding to the students of Greece and philhellenes, but will move others to discover for themselves not only the glory that was Greece but the glory that continues to be Greece.

I am most grateful to all those who took part in the lecture series and kindly contributed their papers for this publication. I wish to record my debt of gratitude to the Friends of the Greek Studies Program of Ball State University for their thirty-year-long generous moral and financial support as well as dedication to the program. In particular, I wish to thank Dr. and Mrs. Philip Ball, Mr. and Mrs. Edmund F. Ball, Mr. and Mrs. Jack E. Buckles, Dr. and Mrs. Richard Burkhardt, Mr. and Mrs. Clell Douglass,

Mrs. Joanna Meeks, Dr. and Mrs. John Pruis, as well as Sir David and Lady Hunt, and Mr. and Mrs. Peter C. Krist. I owe a particular debt of gratitude to Mr. Michael Jaharis, President of The Jaharis Family Foundation, and Ambassador Constantine Leventis, President of The A.G. Leventis Foundation, for generous subventions. Finally, I thank Professor Rosanne Marek, Chair, Department of History, Dr. Ronald L. Johnstone, Dean, College of Sciences and Humanities, and Dr. C. Warren VanderHill, Provost and Vice-President for Academic Affairs of Ball State University for professional assistance in the preparation of the manuscript.

John A. Koumoulides

NOTES

1. Richard Livingstone, Sir (editor), *The Legacy of Greece* (Oxford: Oxford University Press, 1969), p. iv.

2. Moses I. Finley, Sir (editor), *The Legacy of Greece: A New Appraisal* (Oxford: Oxford University Press, 1984). p. iii.

3. Kenneth J. Dover, Sir (editor), *The Greeks and Their Legacy* (Oxford: Basil Blackwell Ltd., 1988), p. vii.

4. Arnold Toynbee, *The Greeks and Their Heritages* (Oxford: Oxford University Press, 1981),

5. John A. Koumoulides (editor), *Greek Connections: Essays on Culture and Diplomacy* (Notre Dame, Ind.: University of Notre Dame Press, 1987).

6. Richard Clogg, "After Independence – Xeniteia: Greeks Outside Greece," in *Greek Civilization: An Introduction*, edited by Brian A. Sparkes (Oxford: Basil Blackwell Ltd., 1998), p. 305.

PART ONE
Ancient Greece

GREECE:
INFLUENCES AND ORIGINALITY

Jasper Griffin

UNTIL VERY RECENTLY we all accepted without much discussion, or much conscious thought, that Ancient Greece was the mother of arts and sciences, the fountain-head of much of our civilization. Recently that easy consensus has been somewhat boisterously challenged: the heritage of Greece has been declared to be a stolen one, derived in truth from sources very different and much further south: from the continent, in fact, of Africa. I have given the public my opinion on these matters already, in the pages of the *New York Review of Books*; and I shall not repeat the arguments that even separately, and much more collectively, render such a view untenable. The question will be glanced at, but not much more. The avid acceptance by so many people of the assertions of Martin Bernal will, I think, be one of the curiosities of intellectual history, a subject for the wonderment of posterity.

Let us begin with the fact, surely not even nowadays controversial, that a long and visible chain of tradition links us and our world with the thought and the achievements of Ancient Greece. At this first stage we can, I think, be content to leave in abeyance the further question of the ultimate source of those thoughts. For the past of the West, they were perceived as the legacy of the Greeks: partly mediated, indeed, through the powerful but often distorting lenses, first of pagan Rome, and then of the Christian Church.

Let us first observe that all of this might have been very different. There are other high traditions in the world. One thinks at once of China and of India: either of them, had history taken another turn—and had geography been more propitious—might have provided the basis of the culture of Europe. To come closer to historical fact, it very nearly did happen that the Arabs, having conquered the homelands of the Christian

3

religion, and having crossed the Pyrenees from Spain into France, succeeded in completing what appeared to be their historic mission by conquering and converting the whole of Europe to Islam. You will recall the urbane comment of Edward Gibbon, that in that case "Perhaps the interpretation of the Koran would now be taught in the schools of Oxford, and her pulpits might demonstrate to a circumcised people the sanctity and truth of the revelation of Mahomet" (Chapter 52). I remark, however, that Greek intellectual influence would not have been disposed of so easily. In that case, too, even in a Europe converted to Islam, the influence of Aristotle, at least, would have continued to be mighty.

However, history in fact took the course that it took. What can we single out as the most important, and most characteristic, features of the tradition that reaches us from Greece? The subject is so enormous that I must proceed rather on the principle of Little Jack Horner. He, you will remember, stuck in his thumb and pulled out a plum (and, in the best tradition of visiting lecturers, did not fail to announce: What a good boy am I!). I, too, shall pull out some plums.

Not least among the legacies of Greece to us is the invention of politics. Of course there had been societies before the rise of the Greek *polis*. What is very hard to find is any hint of the existence of the discussion of the range of possibilities, of forms of government, of the terms on which people might live together in society. I offer as a suggestive contrast the discussion that the Greek historian Herodotus puts into the mouths of a group of high-ranking Persians who have just overthrown a usurping regime and are debating the form of the future constitution. One is for monarchy, one for aristocracy, one (however surprisingly) for that extraordinary Greek invention, Democracy. For democracy the case is that the position of king turns any man into a tyrant, violent and suspicious, arbitrary in action, violating the laws, equally resentful whether he is treated by his subjects with a moderate degree of respect or with exaggerated self-abasement. Democracy, on the other hand, has "the most beautiful of titles, that of equality before the law"; magistrates are answerable to the community for what they do, and decisions are taken after public debate.

The next speaker counters by arguing that while the criticism of monarchy is just, it is even worse to entrust power to the uncontrolled and violent impulses of "a rude unbridled mob"; "a tyrant at least knows what he is doing, but the mass of the people is uneducated and without standards. Let us choose a certain number of the best men and give them the power. For (he concludes, with the true self-confidence of the aristocrat through the ages) we shall ourselves be among the rulers, and it is natural that when power is entrusted to the best men, the best counsels will prevail."

The last speaker finds fault with aristocratic government as productive of rivalries among the elite few, as each strives for supreme power, and so of civil war, leading to the rule of the winner, so that monarchy prevails in the end; while with democracy there inevitably arise criminal conspiracies against the common interest, which in turn provoke the seizure of power by a single champion, to right the wrongs of the system and to make himself supreme on its ruins. If we take the three systems, each in its ideal form, then surely the rule of a single very good man is both more secure and more acceptable than that of either of the other two. And besides, that is the custom of our Persian ancestors (Herodotus iii.80–82).

Now, that may not strike us as the most sophisticated imaginable discussion of the question, and the Greeks were to go on to refine it very considerably; but we see the extraordinary fact that it is possible to discuss, and to choose, among three separate models of the basic structure of society, and to produce arguments about the choice that are, in outline at least, rational. It implies the ability to stand outside the immediate frame of one's own society and to see it as one of a range of potential options. I make the further point, to which we shall return, that Herodotus sets the discussion, not among Greeks, but among Persians: the national enemy, who invaded and tried to conquer their homeland. The discussion is unthinkable as having actually taken place among Iranian grandees in the late sixth century, at a date when democracy had not yet appeared in the world.

Democracy cannot be found among the Persians, or the Babylonians, or the people of ancient Egypt. It has no real predecessors. It starts up quite suddenly, as far as we can see, in Athens, about 500 B.C.; created, perhaps, in part by accident, in the course of party struggles between aristocratic factions, but at once formulated as a procedure and an ideology. Democracy meant equality before the law, for male citizens; open access to office and power; magistrates who held office for a limited term and then were accountable to the citizen body for their actions; and majority decisions, openly arrived at.

Herodotus, it appears, wanted to include a general discussion, and he made a place for it in his *Histories* by projecting contemporary Greek debates to a distant time and place. It is not easy to find anything analogous to this discussion in the Old Testament. I single out an event recorded in I Samuel 8, when the Israelites demanded that the prophet Samuel should, for the first time, give them a king. This is represented as a break with the older arrangement, that authority resided in a holy man, a prophet. The Israelites demand:

> Now make us a king to judge us like all the nations.

This proposal is displeasing to the prophet, and also to God, who reassures Samuel:

> They have not rejected thee, but they have rejected me, that I should not reign over them.

Samuel predicts to the people the greed and arrogance of a king:

> This will be the manner of the king that shall reign over you: he will take your sons and appoint them for himself, for his chariots, and to be his horsemen... and he will take your daughters to be confectioneries, and cooks, and to be bakers. And he will take your fields, and your vineyards, and your oliveyards, even the best of them...

Despite this discouraging prediction the people insist:

> Nay, but we will have a king over us; that we also may be like all the nations; and that our king may judge us, and go out before us, and fight our battles.

It will be seen how different this account is from that of Herodotus. There is no discussion of alternative forms of government, in the ordinary earthly-sense in which monarchy might be contrasted with democracy or aristocracy. Instead we find the overwhelming role of God and his angry and present will; and the question is only whether the single ruler should be a divinely inspired prophet or a king, a ruler indeed of essentially secular type, but still to be chosen and anointed by the holy man. The decision to be made is between being a special people with a unique relation with Yahweh and having a king and being "like all the nations." The option of democracy does not exist, any more than it did in Assyria or in the Egypt of the Pharaohs, where the only choice was between being, or enduring, a just and fatherly monarch and being, or enduring, a violent and oppressive one—a choice that is moral but not political.

The Persian noble who defended democracy praised it because it brought equality before the law, while a king would "set aside the laws of the land." That brings us to another important point. The question of king or no king in the biblical story does not hinge upon the observance or disregarding of the laws. Law is a very Greek preoccupation. We are reminded by another story in Herodotus that Greeks attached importance to it, and that they thought it characteristic of Eastern kingdoms that they did not. In the course of his invasion of Greece King Xerxes held a review of his mighty fleet and army, a force that in size and splendor far outstripped any possible Greek armament. Calling to his side a Greek exile, Demaratus the ex-king of Sparta, he asked him:

> Surely the Greeks will not fight at all against such odds? Especially as they do not even have one ruler over them, who might possibly drive them into battle by the use of terror, and by having men with whips to force them to go forward.

The exiled king replies that Xerxes is sadly mistaken. These are free men indeed, but not completely:

> For they have over them a master, of whom they are much more in awe than your slaves are of you, and that is the Law; and they do its bidding (Herodotus vii.104).

At this obviously ridiculous reply King Xerxes laughed and changed the subject, but of course it turned out to be true.

What is the law? It is not expressed as the Will of God, and it is not obedience to the divine will that is being exalted here as the supreme quality. In democratic Athens it is the laws that are supreme, and the laws are made by men. It is the laws of his country that come and remonstrate with Socrates, in the *Crito* of Plato, when he is in prison, under sentence of death, and tempted to escape and evade his punishment. The law, says Demaratus, is what a man respects and obeys, without becoming a slave.

To think and argue in terms of the law requires a certain habit of abstract thought. So does another central aspect of Greek thinking: the conception of a range of virtues. The word "virtue" is very rare in our English translations of the Bible. One instance comes immediately to mind, when Jesus is brushed in the crowd by a sick woman who is healed by the contact, and feels that virtue is gone out of him (Mark v.30); but it is striking that the Greek word there is not *arete*, "virtue," but *dynamis*, which would be better translated "power." The Old Testament characteristically has little occasion to mention other good qualities than subjection to the will of God, and the New Testament, too, rarely analyzes action or impulse in terms of virtue. The Greeks, in marked contrast, use this vocabulary constantly, and Aristotle in the *Ethics* thinks it a valuable and natural part of a treatise on moral philosophy to analyze and describe in detail the several virtues and their corresponding vices (not, of course, sins: sin is a concept for which the Greeks, in their turn, have little use).

The Greeks of the classical period spoke of four virtues as cardinal: wisdom, justice, courage, and self-control. The Christians add three more, the so-called theological virtues: faith, hope, and charity. For the Greeks hope was not a virtue—hope gets a bad press, as a deceiver, in classical literature—and the sort of faith envisaged by the Christians, if they could have understood it at all, would certainly not have seemed to them to be something laudable. Even the last of the three, charity or love, they would have found puzzling—as perhaps we do, too; witness our difficulty, in St. Paul's First Epistle to the Corinthians, in knowing how to translate the word. Discussion of action in terms of these separate virtues goes with an analytic approach, both to human nature and to moral action, and also, I think, with the belief that people are different, that even good people are not simply all good in the same way, and that there exist many interesting possibilities for behavior and its judgment. It will be seen how far distant such a conception is from that which has normally prevailed outside the range of Greek influence.

I turn to the matter of literature. Greek literature shares with the other arts of classical Greece the quality of keen interest in form and in formal perfection. This is what made the impact of Greek arts on the other peoples of antiquity so devastating. Faced with the refinement and elegance of Greek statues, poems, temples, indigenous artifacts looked unbearably uncouth. One is distantly reminded of the impact of French poetry and prose on educated Germans in the eighteenth century, and on Russians in the nineteenth.

It is one of the most striking features of Greek literature that it falls as if by nature into the different genres—epic, tragedy, comedy, lyric, romance, epithalamium, and so on—which at the Renaissance every European literature felt itself obliged to recreate in its own language. Originally these genres arose in the context of the needs and the pattern of Greek life: the festivals at which plays were staged, the occasions of funeral and wedding that called for dirges and wedding songs, the processions of girls that needed maiden songs, the worship of Dionysos that required dithyrambs, and all the rest.

With the passing of time many of these specific occasions melted into each other or faded away, so that a tragic drama could be written for any occasion or for none, and a wedding song might be composed as a piece of pure poetry, quite divorced from any actual nuptials. Thus the genres survived, as pure literature, the social structure and the specific occasions that had brought them to birth; and the regularity that continued to be expected of them came to be felt as a purely aesthetic matter. It was nonetheless exacting for that, and so it was inevitable that in the end it should come to be felt as a burden. And so we have the Romantic Movement.

Long before that conscious revulsion from the norms of classicism, it had been a feature of early Christian literature, and above all of the Bible, that it entirely failed to conform to classical canons, whether of grammar and style or of literary genre. The Gospels do not fall into any of the classical forms; nor do the Acts of the Apostles. At a later period in France, a country always closer to the classical world than England, the distinction between tragedy and comedy was felt and enforced with a classicizing strictness that was alien to the looser rules and less classical taste of London. To this day a Frenchman who has been brought up on the consistently elevated tragedies of Racine and Corneille finds it difficult, or perhaps impossible, to take seriously, to accept as tragic, the plays of Shakespeare, which despite their orthodox sounding titles (*The Tragedy of Hamlet, Prince of Denmark*; *The Tragedy of King Lear*) obstinately incorporate passages of prose, low characters, horse play, dirty jokes, and other material that could not possibly find admittance to the stricter world of French classical tragedy.

The domination of Greek literary form, then, was felt in different ways and to varying strengths in the vernacular literatures of Renaissance and modern Europe; but felt it was, everywhere. Without it we readers of English should doubtless never have had the epic *Paradise Lost*, and the pastorals of Spenser, and the satires of Donne and Pope (at one remove, these, by way of the Latin), and Gray's *Elegy*, and the picaresque novel, and the poetic drama. Could other ancient literatures, had they been visible in those formative centuries, have been equally fertile for us? The question cannot be conclusively answered; but the Bible, always visible and always read, has been curiously unproductive in fathering imaginative literature in the modern tongues, and the discovery 170 years ago of a substantial Egyptian literature has not yet given rise to anything very much in the literature of the English-speaking world. And so I am inclined to doubt it.

From this whirlwind tour of matters literary I turn to the visual arts. Every people, however unsophisticated or unselfconscious, produces some kind of drawings, carvings, buildings. The Greeks are not the only ones to have risen to the creation of works of high style and accomplishment. But, again, theirs is a tradition that (as it happened) is fundamental to ours. Greek art is unusual, in some respects, among the traditions of the world. It was extraordinarily lifelike—much more so, of course, when the statues had their original paint and coloring; it attached central importance to the representation of the naked human body, in the early period of the male and later also of the female; and it developed stylistically at an unparalleled speed.

The combination of naturalism and nudity presented problems, first to the Romans (who were by no means at ease in the presence of the nude), and then to later Europe. A later pope than Julius II, Michelangelo's patron, notoriously had loincloths added to the splendid nakednesses of the Last Judgment in the Sistine Chapel. The luscious nudes by Titian and Rubens that had been collected by the first Duke of Marlborough were exiled to an outhouse by a later and more prudish Duchess and eventually destroyed by fire. An anxious bishop wrote to the Victorian painter Alma Tadema, after contemplating his Venus, that "For a living artist to exhibit a life-like representation of a beautiful naked woman strikes my inartistic mind as somewhat mischievous." Only the great prestige of antiquity prevented an unambiguous condemnation of all such work; though here, too, not all European countries advanced in step or to exactly the same tune. Paolina Borghese, the sister of Napoleon Bonaparte, had her portrait carved in marble by the great sculptor Canova, reclining almost naked on a chaise lounge. An English lady, shocked, asked her how she could bear to pose so. "Oh," replied the Princess, "there was a good fire in the room." The exquisite result, which surely justifies the insouciance of the lovely sitter, is still to be admired in the Borghese Villa in Rome.

What of the nude in other ancient traditions? The naked goddesses of Mesopotamia seem to have been rather talismans than works of art in the sense of pure aesthetics: quasi-magical creations, intended to help the fertility of the crops, the livestock, and the human worshippers. Their exaggerated female characteristics reinforce that impression: these are not, at least not primarily, objects of beauty. The Aphrodites of later Greece, like their male counterparts the Apollos, embody an aesthetic ideal, divorced from practical function, to be admired for itself. The Hebrews, of course, like the Moslems and like many Christian sects from the ancient world until today, rejected and abhorred such representations altogether.

The acceptance of nudity in Greece spread far beyond the visual arts. Athletics were performed naked; our word *gymnastics* comes from the Greek for "naked." In the fifth century B.C. the Greeks were aware that this was one of the great differences between them and the rest of the world ("the barbarians," as the Greeks called them). "Among the barbarians," writes Herodotus with condescension, "it is thought shameful even for a man to be seen naked, let alone a woman." This sense of being at ease with the body worked with the very strong Greek sense of beauty, and responsiveness to it, to produce a people with an unequalled vocation for the arts. The sense of beauty seems to have been stronger, in some ways, than any religious awe, and it was natural for the Greeks to represent the gods as handsome and splendid men and women; unless it would be still more accurate to speak of them as presenting men and women as gods and goddesses. We see how strong the contrast with other ancient peoples was, when we reflect that in Judaea one of the main causes of the nationalist and traditionalist revolt of the Maccabees, in the second century B.C., was that creeping Hellenism had advanced so far that there was a gymnasium and a wrestling school actually in Jerusalem. That could not be tolerated, and the result was an explosion of Jewish fundamentalism.

Hardly less productive for the arts of the West than the exaltation of the nude, perhaps, was the rapid pace of artistic change. The contrast is unmissable between the immobility of Egyptian art, or the slow development of Romanesque, and the hectic pace of change and innovation in Western art since the Renaissance and the rediscovery of the arts of the classical world.

It is time to turn our attention back to literature, this time from a different point of view. The Homeric poems stand at the very beginning of all the literature of the West. It is true, as we now know since the decipherment of many of the once lost or indecipherable languages of the

Near East, that the *Iliad* and *Odyssey* come out of a long period of inter-action between Greece and the East. From the East the Greeks learned their alphabet and relearned the art of writing, lost for 400 years. It even appears that they learned the names of the letters—in Greek the mean-ingless rigmarole *alpha—beta—gamma—delta*—by listening to the names of the letters being recited in some Semitic school: for in Semitic those sounds are all meaningful. But it is hardly less important that the Greeks transformed the whole business by the crucial innovation of promoting all the vowels to be full letters, written out fully along with the conso-nants, instead of being simply inferred by the reader, who almost has to know what each word is before he can read it. This change produced a uniquely efficient high-tech alphabet, the ancestor of all the Western alphabets, which could be read far more easily than its Eastern predeces-sors; and that in turn made it possible for many more people to learn to read; and *that* meant that writing was much less of a mystery. So the fine new alphabet was partly responsible for the absence in Greece of a closed and powerful class of scribes. Like a powerful class of priests, such a thing did not exist in Greece, a fact with momentous consequences for freedom of speculation.

From the East came also important elements in the mythology that we find in Homer, including such a central idea as that the gods all live together, quarreling and intriguing and feasting together on the top of Mount Olympus. We see them reclining on their clouds, not only in liter-ature (the *Aeneid* of Virgil comes to mind) but also on the ceilings of a thousand churches and libraries and ballrooms and parliaments, all over the West, from Portugal to Russia. Such a conception of the communal life of the gods, even to their living on a mountain "in the North," meets us in the epic poems of the Phoenicians, now that we can read the liter-ature of Ugarit. It is alien to real Greek religion, which did not imagine its gods living all together, or thwarting each other's purposes and opposing each other's favorites. It is of the greatest use for poetry, making possible some lively scenes of divine confrontation, and a splendid complexity in the divine motivation of human actions. But we do not find in the Orient some of the most characteristic notes of Homer: notably the humanity that pervades the poems, insisting on chivalrous treatment of women, for example, and respect for the dead, even if the dead man was in life a hated enemy.

The last books of the *Iliad* concern the furious rage of the great hero Achilles against the corpse of his enemy Hector, the slayer of Achilles' dear friend Patroclus. For days he maltreats the body; for days the gods see to it that the body sustains no real harm. In the end the gods intervene. Not even Achilles, son of a goddess and mightiest of heroes, can do this with impunity; he must surrender the body to Hector's father Priam for burial. The poor old king of Troy comes through the night to the killer of his son, kneels at his feet, kisses his hand. Priam and Achilles weep together, both recognizing that Priam resembles Achilles' own father Peleus, alone and far away, who will never see his son again. All men, says Achilles, must suffer: that is what it is, not to be a god. The national difference of Greek and Trojan shrivels, in that perspective, to insignificance.

Now, at the end and climax of the poem, we see why it was so important that Greeks and Trojans are shown speaking the same language and—still more—praying to the same gods. This is a depiction of war, even against a foreign foe, that is radically different from the writings of the Assyrians or the Hebrews. There what we find is "Assur my lord put into my hand a mighty weapon that subdued the insubmissive"—followed by gruesome accounts of flayings and beheadings and the building of pyramids of skulls; or "The LORD delivered them into the hand of Israel," followed by the complete destruction of the defeated, rejected by God and consigned to annihilation (and woe betide Saul, if he fails to extirpate the Amalekites without trace).

As for respect for the remains of the dead: the king of Assyria dug up the buried remains of the kings of Elam, when he conquered that people, and boasted "I made them more dead than they were before." And in Israel the bad queen Jezebel was thrown down from a window by eunuchs, "and some of her blood was sprinkled on the wall, and on the horses, and Jehu, (the avenger and next king), trode her under foot"; dogs ate her body, except for her skull, and her feet, and the palms of her hands; and those remains were cast out "as dung upon the face of the field" (II Kings 9). We see even now, from horrific events in Bosnia and elsewhere, how hard it is not to pursue vengeance beyond death. To do so was recognized by the Greeks as a terrible temptation.

After the Battle of Plataea a man of Aegina, says Herodotus, came to the Spartan king Pausanias and said, "Look, here is the corpse of the Persian commander Mardonius. You remember what Mardonius and his king Xerxes did to the body of the Spartan king Leonidas after the Battle of Thermopylae: they cut off his head and stuck it on a pole. Now you can do the same to Mardonius, and everyone will praise your action." But Pausanias rose to the occasion. "We leave that kind of thing to barbarians," he replied, "and even in them we regard it with disgust. Never come to me again with such a suggestion; and think yourself lucky that you have got away with it this time" (Herodotus ix.78–79).

It would be possible to expand on this point. It is more than tempting to contrast that splendid piece of early Hebrew poetry, the triumph song of the prophetess Deborah over the death of Sisera, the general of the Canaanite enemy (Judges 5), through whose head, as he slept, a Hebrew woman had driven a tent-peg, with Aeschylus' play *The Persians*, recording the defeat of Xerxes and the Persian host. On the one side, bitterness, gloating, and derision. I quote:

> He asked water, and she gave him milk; she brought forth butter in a lordly dish. She put her hand to the nail, and her right hand to the workmen's hammer; and with the hammer she smote Sisera, she smote off his head, when she had pierced and stricken through his temples. At her feet he bowed, he fell, he lay down; at her feet he bowed, he fell; where he bowed, there he fell down dead. The mother of Sisera looked out at a window, and cried through the lattice, "Why is his chariot so long in coming? Why tarry the wheels of his chariots?" ... So let all thine enemies perish, O LORD...

On the other, a commemoration of the national victory and deliverance that takes the unexpected form of lamentations among the kinsfolk of the defeated, far away in Persia, dignified and moving.

But occasionally a temptation must be resisted, and I shall not linger longer on this poignant contrast. I remark only that the ability to see the enemy as fundamentally human, akin to oneself, not monstrous, and therefore not to be simply exterminated with unmixed gusto, is connected with the idea that they do not worship completely different gods. The Greeks put forward various explanations of that astounding event, their victory in 480–79 B.C. over the invading hordes of the East and Xerxes their king. We find analyses in terms of environmental factors: the soil of Greece is thin, the country has always been poor, and poverty has made us tough, whereas the Asiatics live in lusher territory, where the crops and fruits grow richly with little human effort; and so we Greeks have to grow up tough, while they grow up soft. Another line, related but different, pointed instead to the aspect of places, the direction they face, the

nature of the prevailing winds, the quality of the water, and the bright-
ness or dullness of the air. A bad elevation, a heavy atmosphere, streams
that are not bright and clear: all these predispose the inhabitants to
torpor and feebleness.

Another line of thought, as we have seen, explained the result in
what might be called political terms. We Greeks have the *polis*, we are
citizens, we have the rule of law; whereas the subjects of the Great King
are slaves, at the mercy of his whims and his arbitrary actions. "Among
the barbarians all are slaves but one," says a character in a play of Euripides. There was even a religious line. The Persian kings should have been
content to rule Asia, and God resented the arrogance of their attempt to
conquer Europe as well. But what was missing was an explanation of the
form: Our gods defeated their gods. That is a crucial point of difference.

I should like to connect this state of mind with the Greek invention
of history. Again, there were of course writings about the past before
Herodotus; so what is it that was new? Greeks had been taught, ever
since the *Iliad*, that limitless hatred was not a virtue, that great heroes
could, without ceasing to be heroic, think of their enemies as being like
themselves, worthy objects of courtesy and pity. That was the inescap-
able message of the encounter of Achilles and Priam in *Iliad* xxiv. Both
sides, that is, were to be taken seriously. It is, I think, from that starting
point that it was possible to advance to the idea of a treatment of historical events that should aim to be fair to both sides; to be objective; to be,
in fact, *truthful*.

That meant getting away from the crude jingoism, and also from the
naive wonders, that seem to come so naturally to humankind when they
narrate the deeds and the sufferings of their people. The historian
Macaulay gives us a memorable phrase here, applauding the turn in
Indian historiography, under Western influence, away from "History,
abounding with kings thirty feet high, and reigns thirty thousand years
long—and geography made up of seas of treacle and seas of butter." Both
the fantastic excesses of quasi-mythical storytelling, and also the trium-
phalist theocratic narratives of the Near East, were to be replaced by an
approach that could say of itself that its aim was to preserve in memory
the great deeds of both sides, Greek and non-Greek, alike. I have just
quoted the opening sentence of the *Histories* of Herodotus, who lived up
to his program with such success that later generations of Greeks,
hungry for simple-minded eulogies of Our Finest Hour, denounced him

as "pro-barbarian." History would also increasingly look for the causes of events and actions on the human, not on the divine, plane.

Herodotus himself advanced a great part of the way towards this double goal; we read in his pages of "the divine" and "the God" (or "god"), but there are few divine names and no lively scenes of divine conflict. Less than one generation later Thucydides took the last step and excluded the divine from history completely. His favored types of causation are in terms of economics and the will to power. He is in fact a fine example of a scientific historian of the late nineteenth or early twentieth century, the first example known to us.

His work is in a way the logical end position of a main current of Greek thought, and in the writing of history and the treatment of the past it is one for which we cannot see a precedent anywhere in the West, (or in the South). I mean the drive to understand the world, both human action and also the natural universe, with the role of the divine and the irrational reduced to an absolute minimum. At the same time as Thucydides was wrestling with his economic and political account of recent history, medical writers were working out a theory of disease that should eliminate theology from it. Epilepsy had always been viewed with special alarm and superstitious fears, because of its unpredictable attacks, which had led Greeks to call it the Sacred Disease: such inexplicable fits must surely be the direct work of the supernatural. Up-to-date medical writers of the late fifth century B.C. ridiculed this notion. Epilepsy, they point out firmly, is no more (and no less) sacred than any other disease; and it, too, has intelligible causes.

There were accounts in the air of the workings of the human mind that left no room for the ancient picture of arbitrary divine interventions; the mind was a complex unity, self-motivating and self-governing. Even dreams, that ancient medium to transmit messages from another world, were perhaps caused by purely natural causes, over-eating, or anxiety, or an uncomfortable posture in the bed. Some thinkers denied that the oracular utterances of Delphi and the other religious centers had any supernatural value: Thucydides records as a curiosity, almost with amusement, that an oracle predicting the duration of the great war between Athens and Sparta actually did come true. And there were those who alarmed or enraged the pious by asserting that the sun was not a god but an enormous red hot mass.

I find a story recorded by Martin Buber about a Hasidic rabbi in Eastern Europe in the nineteenth century that well illustrates the particular character of Greek intellectual curiosity and some typical attitudes that are opposed to it. The rabbi is discussing with a pupil the shocking statement of a non-Hasidic Jewish thinker that Aristotle knew more about the heavens than did the prophet Ezekiel. Imagine, says the rabbi, two men who are both summoned to dinner in the royal palace by the king. One, as he walks through the palace, looks curiously into every room he passes and tries to explore everything; the other walks straight forward with only one thought in his mind: that he is coming into the presence of the king. Ezekiel is the latter, and he is the one who should be admired. He is not, clearly, a Greek.

It would be easy for me, but wearisome for you, to go through the various disciplines that the Greeks endeavored to reduce to scientific order and method, from zoology and meteorology to rhetoric and the criticism and emending of texts. Textual criticism was invented in Alexandria to purify the text of the Homeric poems; from that source it was taken over for the study of the texts, first of the Hebrew, and then of the Christian scriptures. The systematic study of grammar was invented separately in two places, in India by Sanskrit scholars, and by Greeks for Greek. The technical terms that they coined for their new study were translated rather literally for the study of the Latin language, with the result that some of them, which we still use perforce, are pretty inappropriate: thus "accusative" as a name for the grammatical case for the direct object of the verb is really unintelligible, except in the light of the Greek of which the Latin "accusativus" is a calque.

Such things serve as small reminders of the fundamental position of Greek technical thought and writing for all the scientific work of the West. It is becoming quite fashionable to criticize, even to sneer at, the methods of rational procedure and systematic analysis that are a great part of our inheritance from Ancient Greece. One can see why. On the one hand, some of the specific discoveries of modern scientific research have turned out to be terrifying. On the other, the whole pace of progress and of change has itself been so speedy, and promises to go on accelerating so fast, that the individual feels exposed and intimidated. We should perhaps, in this late romantic age, be happier to believe that there exist alternative sources of knowledge, less austerely scientific, more warm and moony and mystical, of at least equal value. The tradition that demands proof, evidence, chains of argument, regular procedures, a sound theoretical basis: the tradition that goes back ultimately to the scholars and thinkers of classical Greece: all that is too masculine, too rational. The word is, I believe, *phallogocentric* (though not in Oxford). I am not wholly without sympathy with that view; but it is only right to remind ourselves that the rational method works, it gets results, it has given us inoculation and anaesthetics and airplanes that fly. That is not nothing; and most of us, while we may declaim against its benefits, have no intention of giving them up.

I have said something of the debt of the Greeks to the peoples of the East. What of the South? What, finally, of the exotic black Athena of Egypt, alleged patroness of all the Hellenic arts and sciences? From the strange land of Egypt, sometimes open and sometimes closed to the Greeks, what they derived were not intellectual images but visual ones. What struck them about Egypt was the look of things. It was, in fact, what strikes the tourist today: the vast size of the monuments, and their fathomless and changeless antiquity. Where we see Egyptian influence in early Greece is in the look of the temples and their columns, and above all in the statues. It was clear to the ancients, as it is to us, that the male statues that we call *kouroi*, those familiar figures, standing with one leg advanced, their gaze frontal, their hair hanging down their backs, take their origin from Egyptian statuary.

But step by step, and with surprising speed, the sculptors of Greece developed the pose, made it more supple, more life-like, more various: and finally moved on from it. They escaped from the rigid frontality that continued to characterize Egyptian statues, as long as they went on being made. The development of Greek art is in the sharpest possible contrast with the immobility and immutability of the art of Egypt: an art that went on, for centuries, representing first Macedonian and then Roman rulers in the exact pose, and in the exact style, of the pharaohs of earlier centuries and millennia.

That indeed has always been the appeal of ancient Egypt, for those who have found it fascinating. Its unchanging culture and rigidly hieratic art go with the colossal scale of its monuments, and with the assertion of death over life that is unmistakable in the obsessive concern with embalming the dead, with furnishing their tombs, with providing so scrupulously for the posthumous journey and judgment of the soul. Its great book is the *Book of the Dead*. The one significant contribution of Egypt to Greek literature was the papyrus plant that was their equivalent of paper. Egypt appeals especially to those who hope to survive death, to read off the secrets of past and future from the measurements of primeval pyramids.

When we look at the neo-classical period of the early nineteenth century, we see that while Greek made its appeal to poets and writers and artists, to Shelley and Hölderlin, Goethe and Byron and Delacroix, the influence of Egypt was to be seen in the design of furniture. Chairs and tables, cups and vases, and even the occasional building—that is the sphere of the influence of Egypt. And I think that was no accident. So it was in the ancient world, too. And even, I think, one could say something similar of the present day. The great Egyptian exhibition of a few years ago unleashed a flood of Egyptomania, which took shape in the reproduction of objects: ankhs, and lotuses, and jewelry, and, of course, the beautiful expressionless mask of Tutankhamun—the very essence of a certain unthinking, idealess beauty; the forerunner, we may say, of Antinous, the boyfriend of the Emperor Hadrian, who had the same drowsy sensuous features, and who drowned himself in the Nile; and also of Elvis Presley, in whom that look was reborn. Beautiful, ladies and gentlemen, it is; but with a beauty utterly removed from the vigorous, energetic, and restlessly changing beauty of Greece.

NOT OUT OF AFRICA:
REFLECTIONS ON
THE ORIGINS OF GREEK CIVILIZATION

Mary R. Lefkowitz

WHAT ARE THE ORIGINS of ancient Greece? Until very recently there was little interest in this question, because everyone thought they knew at least the basic answers. The people we now call the Greeks (they called, and still call themselves Hellenes) had settled on the Greek mainland and in the Aegean by the early second millennium B.C. Because the language that they spoke was Indo-European, it was assumed that their first origins were in the Indian sub-continent. We know very little about the previous inhabitants of the region; their culture or cultures seem to have been replaced by or absorbed into what we now think of as Greek culture. There seemed to be no reason to think that the achievements of the ancient Greeks were borrowed or stolen from any other civilization. Comparison with documents in Sanskrit and other Indo-European languages suggests that they brought with them, along with their version of the parent language, some ideas about poetry and myth (Watkins 1995). But they were also influenced over a period of many centuries by neighboring civilizations in the ancient Mediterranean. It would have been remarkable had the ancient Greeks not been subject to such influences. The Greeks were always in communication with many different peoples, among them the Phoenician, Hittites, and Egyptians. Greek culture was improved by contributions from each of these ancient civilizations, and in recent years the connections among them have been studied and explored (Lloyd 1991, 281–98; Burkert 1992, 120–27).

But recently it has been claimed that the debt of ancient Greek culture to one of these neighboring cultures (at best) has been not fully understood, and (at worst) deliberately ignored. That is the relation of ancient Greece with ancient Egypt. Why this new concern? Has there been a major archaeological discovery that suggests Greece was colonized

20

from Egypt? Has Greek language been shown to be closely akin to Egyptian? Have documents been discovered that reveal close similarities between ancient Egyptian texts and writings that have always been thought to have originated in Greece? Although no scholar in the several fields of ancient Mediterranean studies has made such a suggestion, the question is nonetheless being asked with increasing insistence. The suggestion that the achievements of ancient Greece were borrowed from Africa comes from outside the field, from two different but closely related sources.

The primary inspiration for the idea comes from a group of writers of African descent, who do not claim to be experts in the field of ancient Mediterranean studies, but rather wish to demonstrate that the achievements of African civilizations, and especially that of ancient Egypt, have been ignored or wrongly characterized by people of European descent. For many years these ideas were not well known outside of the African-American community, but after 1987 they became the subject of increased interest within the academy as the result of the publication of the first volume of Martin Bernal's multi-volume project *Black Athena: The Afro-Asiatic Roots of Classical Civilization*. In his first volume, *The Fabrication of Ancient Greece 1785–1985*, Bernal, a Sinologist who is a professor of Political Science at Cornell University, sought to show that classical scholars had downplayed the debt of Greece to Egypt and the Near East out of racism and anti-Semitism. In volume II, *The Archaeological and Documentary Evidence*, published in 1991, Bernal attempted to provide the hard data to support his assertions. Although it is fair to say that few (if any) scholars in the field were persuaded by the arguments in the second volume, his discussions in the first volume of the racism and anti-Semitism in Classical scholarship gave his views much more weight than they might have had in a period of history where issues of race were not at the forefront of public concern (Levine 1992; Lefkowitz and Rogers 1996, x–xi).

In particular, Bernal's ideas have found wide acceptance among those who seek to rewrite ancient history from an "Afrocentric" perspective, and so are eager to assert that *Black Athena* provides the intellectual underpinnings for some earlier African-American theories about the debt of Greece to ancient Egypt. As a result, these theories have made their way into courses in universities and schools throughout this country (Martel 1996; Ortiz de Montellano 1996; Lefkowitz 1997, 239–41).

Young people are now being taught that the name Athena was derived from the Egyptian goddess Neith and that Greek philosophers such as Pythagoras, Socrates, and Plato learned about philosophy at universities in Egypt that were affiliated with an "Egyptian Mystery System." Many also are told that Aristotle stole Egyptian books from the library at Alexandria and passed them off as his own when he got back to Athens.

The proponents of such "Stolen Legacy" theories about the "theft" of Egyptian ideas by ancient Greeks do not start from the premise that their students should learn all they can about the languages and histories of the two ancient civilizations. Rather, they encourage their students to ignore the work of most scholars of European descent, on the grounds that it is "Eurocentric" and thus by definition biased against "Afrocentrism," because each nation or ethnicity will write history in order to promote its own particular values. Since as a result (or so the argument goes) the history written by one group will automatically be invalid for another, there is no reason to trust the work of scholars in the traditional fields of ancient Mediterranean Studies. Instead, the revisionists feel justified in insisting that their students study a limited set of approved books that convey a considerable amount of misinformation. Anyone who insists that a large quantity of evidence has simply been overlooked by the writers of these books can be contemptuously dismissed as racist, or at the very least, a Eurocentric promoter of the "purity" of Greek civilization. I myself have been called (among other things) a typical Jewish agitator, an Aryan conspirator, a conservative, a Luddite, a racist, and an author of a "racist discourse" (Lefkowitz 1997a).

But since these assertions, and others like them, have had and will continue to have a noticeable effect on education in the United States, it is important for scholars in the fields of Classics and Egyptology to be familiar with them and to discuss them using all the evidence at their command. It should be stated at the outset that the purpose of the discussion should not simply be to scrutinize these claims, and, when and if such criticism is justified, to demonstrate why many of them are exaggerated or unfounded. We need also to ask why it is that intelligent people seek to believe such claims, even though many of them fly in the face of scientific evidence. In other words, we need to look at the reasons why the notion arose that the ancient Greeks stole or borrowed significant aspects of their culture from ancient Egypt, because this notion is an important cultural phenomenon that needs to be better understood than it has been so far, especially by scholars of the ancient Mediterranean.

In this essay I will attempt to explain the motives behind the Afrocentric theory of antiquity and the reasons for its creation. But I will also try to show that although the question of the relation between Greek and Egyptian culture is interesting and well worth pursuing in detail, the way in which it is now being pursued does not advance knowledge or encourage students to become better informed about antiquity. As I have sought to show in my book, *Not Out of Africa*, there is in fact little evidence to support the most insistent claims now being made. The name Athena does not derive from Neith (Jasanoff and Nussbaum in Lefkowitz-Rogers 1996, 193–94). The Egyptian Mystery System that some Afrocentrist writers believe to be the precursor of Greek philosophy is in fact a purely European creation, invented by an eighteenth-century French priest, who took his ideas from Greek and Roman sources. (He had of course no other choice, since no one knew about the real intellectual life of Egypt until the nineteenth century, when hieroglyphics were deciphered, and Egyptian inscriptions and papyri could be read.) Aristotle could not have stolen books from the library at Alexandria, because the library was not built until after his death.

My interest in discussing the historical evidence for these and other claims is not motivated by cultural chauvinism. I do not regard ancient Greek civilization as a sacred preserve, or consider the ancient Greeks to be less subject to outside influences than other peoples. On the contrary, I wish only to describe what happened in the past as accurately as possible. Considering these issues has caused me to reexamine all my assumptions about the connections between ancient Egyptian and Greek cultures. As a result of this study I am persuaded that Egyptologists and Classicists have not been guilty of any intentional or unintentional attempts to conceal any evidence that might be germane to the discussion, and that they have provided an accurate general assessment on the basis of what now can be known. But I also believe that we should continue to ask if we have yet described as accurately as we can the extent of cultural influence between ancient Egypt and ancient Greece (remembering, of course, that cultural influence almost always is a two-way process). We may find that scholars have overvalued Egyptian art at the expense of other Egyptian cultural achievements, such as their complex theology, and that they have not fully explored the connections of ancient Egypt to other ancient African civilizations.

I became interested in this controversy about Greek origins because I have always been interested in mythical history. The ancients, when writing about the remote or even the immediate past, did not have the exhaustive resources that we now have at their disposal for their research. As a result they were compelled to rely on hearsay and tradition, which more often than not was what we now call myth and legend. Even great historians such as Herodotus and Thucydides relied on mythical patterns when constructing the framework of their narratives, and lesser writers, whose names have long since been forgotten, would on occasion create fictional narratives of the past, using the structures of myth, conjecturing details and motives on the basis of "likelihood" (*eikos*) (Lefkowitz 1983). The detailed, sometimes quite lengthy lives of the famous Greek epic and dramatic poets are based almost entirely on information gleaned from their own poetry, even though that poetry, by its nature, provides little or no real biographical information. In my own work on these lives, I sought to learn not only how the biographers constructed their narratives, but also *why* they wrote such mundane biographies that told us so little about the nature of the writers' art. I concluded that they often sought to make these great authors into ordinary, even pathetic people, even though, or perhaps because they had been regarded as geniuses and, in some cases, even worshiped as heroes in their own cities. The mythologizing process thus had for the biographers and their audiences an important social function: it made them feel more comfortable and even to be able to look down on these men and women of genius by reducing and even demeaning the stature of the individual poets (Lefkowitz 1981).

It may seem as though the ancient lives of Greek poets would have little to do with modern Afrocentrist history, but in fact there are some important similarities. In constructing their own narrative of the past, Afrocentrist writers have sought to transform that past into something that serves their particular purposes. The myth that they have constructed speaks about the greatness of African achievement, and belittles the Greek and European contribution to the development of philosophy and science. It says, in effect, that anything that the ancient Greeks were supposed to have been able to do could and was also done by ancient African peoples. And if Africans then (and now) can do what Europeans can do, why is it that African peoples have been treated so appallingly by

European peoples? The myth, then, like all real myths, has a religious function, that is, it attempts to explain and account for a phenomenon that is seemingly beyond everyone's control, the fact of racism.

I share the goal of eliminating racism and support the message of the myth, which says that Africans and people of African descent should be able to do anything that Europeans can do and have done. Nor should any of us disagree with another goal of Afrocentrism, which is to eliminate the widespread ignorance of Africa in this country, and to make sure that all children, not just African-American children, know something about Africa. The myth also speaks to another pervasive problem, the automatic assumption that European civilization (however that may be defined) is superior to all others. Instead, the myth encourages us to realize that all peoples have something to teach other peoples. It reminds us that Egypt is in Africa and the ancient Egyptians were an African people—a view that is supported by most Egyptologists and anthropologists. There is no evidence that the population of ancient Egypt was not indigenous (Keita 1993; Roth 1996, 313–19; Brace 1996, 159). When Herodotus says that being dark-skinned and woolly-haired were Egyptian characteristics, why should we doubt his eyewitness testimony? Another positive feature of the Afrocentrist myth of antiquity is that it reminds us that the intellectual achievement of ancient Egypt may have been undervalued by Europeans. Afrocentrism urges us to look at ancient Mediterranean civilizations from a new perspective, and to that extent is instructive for all students of the ancient world. If it achieves nothing else, the Afrocentric myth of antiquity has brought and will continue to bring new vitality to the study of ancient Egyptian civilization (Roth 1996, 326).

But significant problems arise when this myth, like any other, is substituted for history. First of all, it draws much of its force from unchallenged assumptions about culture, such as its characterization of European civilization, which can only be maintained at the highest level of generality. The notion that there is such an entity as "Europe," with its many cultures and languages, is as artificial as the notion of an "Africa," with its even greater diversity of civilizations and human speech. The Afrocentrist myth, with its suggestion that ancient Egypt somehow stands for the rest of Africa, oversimplifies the situation greatly. The ancient Egyptians were a civilization on the continent of Africa, with ties to other African civilizations, especially those located to the south and east. But they were also in communication, and involved in conflict with civilizations in the Near East. They were widely separated from sub-Saharan Africa by geography and language. Although it is easier to talk about ancient Egypt than other great African civilizations, because they left a written as well as a monumental legacy, concentration on Egypt allows us to ignore other great African civilizations, such as that of Benin, which also deserve to be studied for their own sakes.

But there is another equally serious drawback to the Afrocentric myth, and that is its openly negative message. It is almost as if the myth were designed to impose a reverse racism, to turn the tables on the European values that have done so much harm to peoples of African descent. In its most radical form the myth seeks to make ancient Greek civilization appear to be insignificant and culturally inferior to other ancient civilizations. The principal source of the extreme form of the myth is *Stolen Legacy*, by George G. M. James. The book was first published in 1954, but has been reprinted many times. There may be as many as half a million copies in circulation (Lefkowitz 1997, 254). James characterized the ancient Greeks not only as plagiarists and robbers, but as a people who "did not possess the native ability essential to the development of philosophy," because of their contentiousness, hostility to foreign ideas, and general poverty (James 1954, 163–64). One of James's primary goals was to remove ancient Greece from its cultural pedestal and to condemn the praise given to ancient Greece in popular culture on the grounds that such praise has "blind-folded the world, and has laid the foundations for the deplorable race relations of the modern world" (James 1954, 156).

Not only does the Afrocentrist myth require that we regard ancient Greece quite unfairly as the *fons et origo* of one of this country's most compelling social problems. It also requires its adherents to accept as real a profoundly anachronistic and inaccurate notion of ancient Egyptian civilization, because the Egyptian culture portrayed in the myth derives almost exclusively from European sources. As I believe I have demonstrated conclusively in *Not Out of Africa*, the Afrocentrist notion of Egypt derives primarily from Masonic myth and ritual (Lefkowitz 1997, 106–21. These rituals were developed in Europe in the second half of the eighteenth century. They were quickly adopted by settlers in this country, and they also were taken up (although in separate lodges) by people of African descent who had been brought to this continent and to the West Indies (Lefkowitz 1997, 131–34, 251–52; Allen 1996, 7). Although these Masonic rituals were purported to be very ancient, in fact they were based on the portrayal of Egypt in *Séthos*, an eighteenth-century French historical novel. The author of the novel, the Abbé Jean Terrasson, based his work on the only information about Egypt that was then available to him, the texts of ancient Greek and Roman authors. Father Terrasson used the information at his disposal to create an imaginary portrait of Egyptian religious and cultural training, which he assured his readers had been the model for Greek religion and philosophy. This system of training also addressed the educational needs of Father Terrasson's own day. His invention, the Egyptian Mysteries, were a set of demanding initiation rites for Egyptian priests, which tested both their characters and their knowledge. Father Terrasson's contemporaries regarded the Egyptian Mystery system described in the novel as basically historical, despite its obvious anachronisms. The rituals depicted in the novel were incorporated into the rites and even into the architecture of eighteenth-century Freemasonry (Lefkowitz 1997,106–21; Curl 1994, 134–36; Vidler 1987, 83–102; Curl 1991, 136–68).

Most ironically, then, the Afrocentrist myth offers as a model of an ancient African civilization a fictional creation that is substantially European in its most significant elements. Afrocentrist Egypt is also almost incredibly one-dimensional. It seems to have had no bad features, and none of the limitations of knowledge otherwise characteristic of ancient societies: all arts, all sciences, all philosophy had already reached perfection. Some Afrocentrists have even claimed that there was no slavery in ancient Egypt, although there is considerable evidence to the contrary, dating from the earliest times (Loprieno 1997). Others insist that Greek art simply copies Egyptian art (e.g., Asante 1996, 70), as if it were not possible for even a beginning student of art to distinguish between them. Of course it is possible to sympathize strongly with this desire to create a utopia, a Golden Age from which African civilization has fallen, as the result of the deceptive practices of Europeans, ancient and modern. But even though all of us can understand what the myth is trying to tell us, and recognize the reasons why it has such appeal, we cannot forget that it is substantially unhistorical.

If we agree with the ultimate goal of the myth, which is to restore respect for African cultures, shouldn't we allow it to serve as the kind of "noble lie" (*gennaion pseudos*, 414b–c) that Socrates in Plato's *Republic* suggests be used to explain the ordering of social groups in his imaginary ideal state? As usual, no one in Plato's dialogue offers any serious opposition to Socrates' proposal. But I think we should resist the temptation to tell even a "noble lie," particularly in the context of education. This particular lie is not merely untrue; it is also not particularly noble. It is not noble because it credits some people with achievements that they never performed, and falsely accuses others of crimes that they did not commit. Reverse racism is still a form of racism, and as such ought to be rejected by everyone, including the Afrocentrists. Perhaps it is not surprising that they have so far refused to do so; as Socrates points out in Plato's dialogue *Crito* (49d–c), one can agree to a proposition in the abstract, without being able to accept that it might apply to the problems that one is directly concerned with.

Once we fully understand the purpose of the Afrocentric myth, it becomes easier to understand why so far it has been almost impossible to discuss the historical issues that the myth urges us to reconsider. The myth has a moral purpose, and casts its *dramatis personae* in the role of heroes and villains. Therefore, it is necessary for the proponents of the myth to talk of stealing or "massive" (Bernal 1987, 38) borrowing rather than of influence or cultural exchange. The need for easily identifiable heroes and villains explains why the proponents of the myth regularly insist that scholarship is invariably politicized and speak of classicists as if they were intellectual colonialists, determined to invade the territory of the past and to exploit it mercilessly for their own particular purposes. Thus, before we can even begin to approach the historical issues, we need to show that these characterizations are not (except in a few extraordinary circumstances) accurate or fair.

Let us consider first the metaphors of stealing or borrowing, which make it appear that the discussion is about tangible objects rather than about ideas. The metaphor obscures an important difference: if I borrow your car, you do not have it until I return it; if I borrow your *ideas*, you still have your ideas to keep and use, whatever it is that I go off and choose to do with them. The metaphor obscures the fact that cultural influence (unlike stealing or borrowing) is most often an interactive process, with both sides to some degree being influenced by the other. Similarly, the metaphor of colonialism makes it appear that scholars characteristically invade and capture the past, and then do what they want with it. But again the metaphor obscures an important difference in the types of "territory" it is talking about. If Corinth *colonizes* Syracuse, Athens cannot acquire it without a fight. But if a scholar *writes* about Syracuse, there is nothing to prevent other scholars from writing about Syracuse, correcting the first scholar and improving on what he or she has done. Unlike colonists, scholars do not form themselves into armies; in fact, they seem reluctant to work in concert except when they need expert advice. As a result, any fashion in scholarship, although supported by some, will soon be discarded by others. Since opinions are always changing, especially when new evidence comes to light, the notion of scholarship proposed in the Afrocentric myth seems to bear little relation to reality. If there were significant evidence that Greek philosophy was formulated first in Egypt, or that there had been an invasion of Greece by Egypt in the second millennium, or that a large number of Greek words derived from Egyptian, it is not at all likely that scholars would have agreed among themselves to conceal it. Why wait for an outsider like Martin Bernal to come along to reveal the truth that some of their colleagues had tried to conceal? Someone within the field would certainly have been eager to get credit for such a remarkable set of discoveries, had there been any real evidence to support them.

Another problem of definition concerns the word "philosophy." If we use it as the ancients did, it applies to all kinds of knowledge, and therefore anyone who has acquired learning of any kind can be a "philosopher," a lover of wisdom. In that sense all the wisdom literature in the Bible, such as the Book of Proverbs, is "philosophy," and so is the wisdom literature that has come down to us from Egypt, such as the genre of poems known as "Teachings," instructions by a father to a son, with advice about life and ethical problems (Parkinson 1997, 203–83). According to this definition, ancient Greek didactic poems, such as Hesiod's *Theogony* and *Works and Days*, would also count as "philosophy." No one can deny that the ancient Egyptians, Hebrews, and Babylonians (and other ancient peoples, whether or not they used systems of writing) had "philosophy" in this broader sense.

But of course the term "philosophy" can also be used in a more specialized sense, to mean the study of causes and laws underlying reality, or a system of inquiry designed specifically to study those laws and causes. This specialized notion of philosophy was invented, so far as anyone knows, by the ancient Greeks and has no analogue in any other early civilization. The ancient Egyptians, Babylonians, and Hebrews were learned, and had what we would now call advanced civilizations; they could have developed an abstract terminology for discovering causes and principles had they chosen to do so. But they did not study and analyze the nature of reality in abstract, non-theological language. Their writings differ in form as well as in content from the dialogues of Plato, where the argument is presented sequentially, and agreement elicited from an inter-locutor before the discourse can proceed to the next stage of discussion. Thus, when James states in *Stolen Legacy* that the essence of some of Aris-totle's philosophical principles derive from an Egyptian document now known as the Memphite theology, he has overlooked some important distinctions in genre. The Egyptian text gives an account of the work of the god Ptah; Aristotle discards traditional mythology and expresses himself in abstract and impersonal terms (Lefkowitz 1997, 140–41). Although the thoughts expressed in mythical languages in the Memphite theology could be called philosophy in the most general sense of the term, they cannot be called "philosophy" in the more particular sense of the word that is used to describe the works of Plato or Aristotle; if they can, then there is no reason not to regard the first chapter of the Book of Genesis as philosophy, and allege that Aristotle got his ideas from there. If there had been the kind of extensive Egyptian cultural influence on ancient Greece that the Afrocentrists claim, we would expect to find evidence of their existence in Egyptian civilization, such as parallel texts, or direct echoes, as we do in the case of the Roman poets who from early times adapted and quoted Greek sources. But that is precisely what we do not find—in Egypt or anywhere else in the ancient Mediterranean—in the area of what is thought of as Greek philosophy. There is nothing in surviv-ing Egyptian literature that resembles the dialectical methods and argu-mentative structures that Greek philosophers invented. I do not mean to say that the Egyptians were irrational and the Greeks rational, or that the Egyptians did not possess a profound theology and concept of justice, or that this theology and other wisdom is not expressed in surviving Egyp-tian literature; it is simply that Egyptian (or Hebrew) wisdom literatures are essentially different in nature and form of expression from the philo-sophical writings of Plato and Aristotle, which are non-dogmatic and rati-ocinative in character.

But what are we to make of the stories that the Greek philosophers and poets studied in Egypt, which are understood by Afrocentrists to be literally true. There is in fact no reason why Greek intellectuals should not have come to Egypt in the sixth century. Psamtik II (Herodotus' "Psam-metichus") had employed Greek mercenaries in his army and some of them certainly learned to speak Egyptian (Burstein 1995, 106; Bresciani 1997, 248). But there is no contemporary written evidence to suggest that Greeks went to Egypt during this period for purposes other than commerce, and (as I have suggested in *Not Out of Africa*) the "evidence" for cultural exchange cited by later Greek writers seems based on hypothesis or is mistaken altogether (Lefkowitz 1997, 53–90). For example, the Greek historian Herodotus, who travelled to Egypt in the mid-fifth century, says that the Greek holy man and philosopher Pythagoras learned from the Egyptians about the transmigration of souls, but in fact the Egyptians did not believe in transmigration (Lefkowitz 1997, 67–69). The Greek historian Diodorus, who visited Egypt in the mid-first century B.C., states that Solon used Egyptian models for several of his laws; but, again, the suggestion seems to have been based on vague analogy rather than actual contact (Lefkowitz 1997, 75–76, 245–46). The reasons why Greek intellectuals went to Egypt were invented by historians and biographers considerably after their own times. These later writers seem to have imagined that Greek philosophers went to Egypt and to the Near East not to see the world or to acquire wealth but to learn "Eastern Wisdom."

Plato mentions Egypt frequently in his dialogues, and later writers say that he studied there with priests. This information is considered by Afrocentrist writers to be important evidence of Plato's dependence on Egyptian ideas. But the situation is not as straightforward as they have made it appear. If Plato went to Egypt, it is curious that neither he nor any of his contemporaries mention it. And even if he had gone there, what he would have learned there would not have been philosophy in the restricted sense of the term. If an extensive corpus of such philosophical work had existed in Egypt, either in oral or written form, Plato himself or some of his contemporaries would have known about it, and they would have had no reason *not* to acknowledge its existence or no motivation not to boast about their knowledge. Greeks tended to be so respectful of Egyptian learning that they were always eager to use it whenever and wherever they could. But the kind of Egyptian "learning" that Plato refers to in his works takes the form of "wisdom" narratives, that is, the kind of moral tales that we still possess Egyptian examples of. In the *Phaedrus* and the *Philebus* Socrates tells a story about the god Theuth's invention of letters; in the *Timaeus* and in the incomplete dialogue *Critias* Plato has Critias tell the story of Atlantis, which his ancestor Solon learned from an

Egyptian priest during his visit to the Egyptian pharaoh Amasis. These stories are told not in the usual question-and-answer dialogue form, but as long didactic narratives, almost certainly of Plato's own invention (Rutherford 1995, 288–90; Lefkowitz 1997, 189–90, 246). In view of the way Plato uses Egyptian lore, it is misleading to insist that the presence of these tales in his dialogues indicates that he studied in Egypt, especially if by philosophy we mean a system of non-theological and non-dogmatic *argumentation*.

It should by now be clear that by trying to create between Egypt and Greece a closer relationship than scholars have traditionally acknowledged, the proponents of the Afrocentrist myth are determined to give Egypt credit for Greek achievements, and to make Egypt, rather than Greece, the civilization that gets the credit for the development of philosophy and science. So far so good. But if Egypt, an African civilization, played this role in world history, then isn't Egypt also responsible for the negative side of European culture? And once this African civilization becomes the origin of European civilization, then the perceived opposition between Africa and Europe disappears. That outcome is ironical enough, but for the purposes of understanding ancient Africa there is an even greater problem. That is, of course, that the ancient Egypt of the Afrocentric myth is a basically European creation, with European thought structures and European values. Far from informing us about the African nature of ancient Egyptian civilization, the Afrocentric myth most unfortunately keeps us from understanding what is most distinctive and unfamiliar about ancient Egyptian culture. In other words, it keeps us from recognizing the very ideas from which all of us stand to learn the most, because they would inform us about concepts and practices that did not exist in Europe. It is the myth's Eurocentricity, then, that provides the best reason for recognizing that the Afrocentric theory of antiquity is not history, because it keeps us from learning about the real ancient Egypt. What was designed as a means to an Afrocentric education in fact offers an insurmountable obstacle to that goal.

If and when it is possible to move away from the myth and to turn to the study of real ancient Egypt, there is much interesting work ahead of us. A fuller assessment needs to be made of the extent of the connections of ancient Egypt with Nubia and other African civilizations (see Burstein 1996). It is not appropriate for me, since I am not an Egyptologist, to describe what is most important for classicists to learn about Egyptian culture, but I can say that Egyptian ideas of death and of metamorphosis are more complex than their Greek analogues, and well worth investigating for that reason, if for no other. When it comes to tracing instances of Egyptian influence on Greek culture, our task is more difficult, except in the case of art, where an Egyptian inspiration is evident and has long been recognized. But when it comes to influence that involves the use of language, it is more difficult to find close analogues, especially in what we think of now as "high" culture. Even when Greeks were living in Egypt, after Alexander's conquest, cultural exchange on this level is much less evident than might have been expected. Some Egyptians learned Greek, because that was the language of the government, but there was less impetus for Greeks to learn Egyptian. Cleopatra VII was the first Ptolemaic pharaoh to learn the language of the country she ruled. Egyptian loanwords in Greek are all specific and practical; many introduced because no appropriate Greek word could be found, such as *baris* (an Egyptian river boat) or *herpis* (Egyptian wine) (Wiedemann 1883). In areas where one might expect cooperation, such as in the use of magic, cultural exchange also appears to have been limited. Both Egyptians and Greeks used magic spells to affect the outcome of events in their lives, but even during this later period, they used magic words quite differently in their incantations, with the Greeks relying more on sound effects, and the Egyptians on the written word or sign on amulets (Frankfurter 1994, 198). Each regarded the other's language from a distance, and treated it with the kind of respect accorded to incantations. Greeks considered Egyptian writing magical, and (as we know from Horapollo's treatise) erroneously regarded hieroglyphs as sacred symbols. The Egyptians in their turn accorded respect to the power of Greek vowel sounds, perhaps because of their effectiveness; the vowels made it possible to pronounce Greek writing with greater precision than was possible with Egyptian (Frankfurter 1994, 202–3). Greeks had always been drawn by the exoticism of Egypt, which was at once older, wiser, and more primitive, but always, it seems, preferred to gaze upon it from outside. As for Plato in the fourth century B.C., Egyptian atmospherics were sufficient. When Hellenized Egyptians (or Egyptianized Hellenes) wrote for a Greek audience, they could borrow Egyptian external conventions, such as the teaching of a father to a son. The books of Hermes, composed perhaps in the second century A.D., have an analogue in a demotic Egyptian text that was in circulation at the same time but may have been available as early as the first century B.C. This text, like the Greek books of Hermes, has two interlocutors, the god Thoth and a pupil; the god Thoth was identified by the Greeks with their god Hermes. But the Hermes books despite the similarities of their settings, remain resolutely Greek in concept and mode of expression (Lefkowitz 1997, 102–3, 249). The Egyptian theology and highly metaphorical style of the Book of Thoth would have been incomprehensible in a cultivated Greek ambience (Frankfurter forthcoming; Jasnow-Zauzich forthcoming, 12). The extended narratives in Greek novels may have been inspired by Egyptian stories, but we know of only one case where Egyptian material appears to have been translated and incorporated into a Greek format, the Nectanebo episode in the Alexander Romance (Jasnow 1997, 102–3).

Even in the case of Egyptian influence in spheres such as medicine, there are real problems of chronology, with gaps of many centuries between analogous items or practices. Here it appears that while the Greeks took over from the Egyptians specific remedies and practices (von Staden 1989, 1–31), they also invented explanatory theories of their own, not all of which were good. Egyptian doctors treated the womb through all the orifices of a woman's body. Greek doctors, relying on logical deduction rather than on physical examination, hypothesized that the womb could become dislocated in the woman's body and needed to be brought back to its proper place by application of force or medicines (Merskey-Potter 1989, 751–53). One treatment, which involved the application of animal excrement, almost certainly was suggested to them by Egyptian practitioners, who used human excrement to cure women's diseases (von Staden 1992, 18–19). In the case of scientific discovery, the question of influence is complicated, because Egypt was not the only ancient Mediterranean civilization with which the Greeks came into contact. While it is certainly true that the Egyptians and other peoples had knowledge of medicine, mathematics, and astronomy long before the Greeks, the Greeks nonetheless made their own contribution and developed new theoretical formulations that scientists have relied on since that time.

Will it be possible to discuss the question of Egyptian influence on Greek culture without the rancor and distrust that discussion of ancient African civilization almost always seems to generate? I believe that the current controversy is the first important step in that direction. But if progress is to be made, the discussion must be carried on by scholars who have the necessary basic qualifications, specifically knowledge of the requisite ancient languages, literatures, and civilizations. As I have tried to suggest in this lecture, too much distrust has already been generated by misunderstanding, ignorance, and oversimplification. We need to remember that the purpose of studying the past is not primarily to discover our real or supposed origins; it is to find out, so far as we can, what happened in the past. We owe it to the peoples of ancient Egypt and ancient Greece to keep their memory alive, and we can do that best by representing them not as what we want them to be, but as who and what they were.

BIBLIOGRAPHY

Allen, Ernest, Jr. 1996. "Religious Heterodoxy and Nationalist Tradition: The Continuing Evolution of the Nation of Islam," *The Black Scholar* (26. 3-4 Fall/ Winter): 1-34. **Asante, Molefi Kete.** 1996. "Ancient Truths," *Emerge* (7.9, July/ August): 66-70. **Bernal, Martin.** 1987. *Black Athena: The Afroasiatic Roots of Classical Civilization*. Vol. I: *The Fabrication of Ancient Greece*. Rutgers, N.J.: Rutgers University Press; 1991. *Black Athena: The Afroasiatic Roots of Classical Civilization*, Vol II: *The Archaeological and Documentary Evidence*. Rutgers, N.J.: Rutgers University Press. **Brace, C. Loring, *et al.*** 1996. "Clines and Clusters versus 'Race'," in Lefkowitz-Rogers 1996: 129-64. **Bresciani, Edda.** 1997. "Foreigners," in Donadoni 1997: 221-53. **Burkert, Walter.** 1992. *The Orientalizing Revolution: Near Eastern Influence on Greek Culture in the Early Archaic Age*, translated by M. E. Pinder and W. Burkert. Cambridge, Mass.: Harvard University Press. **Burstein, Stanley M.** 1995. *Graeco-Africana: Studies in the History of Greek Relations with Egypt and Nubia*. New Rochelle, N.Y.: Aristide Caratzas. **Curl, James Stevens.** 1991. *The Art and Architecture of Freemasonry: An Introductory Study*. London: B.T. Batsford; 1994. *Egyptomania, The Egyptian Revival: A Recurring Theme in the History of Taste*. Manchester: Manchester University Press. **Donadoni, Sergio,** editor. 1997. *The Egyptians*, and translated by Robert Bianchi, Anna Lisa Crone, Charles Lambert, and Thomas Ritter. Chicago: University of Chicago Press. **Frankfurter, David.** 1994. "The Magic of Writing and the Writing of Magic," *Helios* 21.2: 189-221; (forthcoming). *Religion in Roman Egypt: Assimilation and Resistance*. Princeton: Princeton University Press. **Gross, Paul R., Norman Levitt, and M. W. Lewis,** editors. 1996. *The Flight from Science and Reason*, Annals of the New York Academy of Sciences. Vol. 775. New York: New York Academy of Sciences. **James, George G. M.** 1954. *Stolen Legacy*. New York: Philosophical Library. **Jasanoff, Jay H.**

and Alan Nussbaum. 1996. "Word Games," in Lefkowitz-Rogers 1996: 177–205. **Jasnow, Richard and Theodor Zauzich.** (forthcoming). "A Book of Thoth?" 1–12. **Keita, S. O. Y.** 1993. "Studies and Comments on Ancient Egyptian Biological Relationships," *History in Africa* 20: 129–54. **Lefkowitz, Mary.** 1981. *The Lives of the Greek Poets.* Baltimore: Johns Hopkins University Press; 1983. "Patterns of Fiction in Ancient Biography," *American Scholar* (Spring): 205–18; 1997. *Not Out of Africa: How Afrocentrism Became an Excuse to Teach Myth as History.* Revised Paperback Edition. New York: Basic Books; 1997a. "Not Out of Africa, Revisited," *Times Literary Supplement* (6/20/1997): 15–16. **Lefkowitz, Mary and Guy MacLean Rogers,** editors. 1996. *Black Athena Revisited.* Chapel Hill: University of North Carolina Press. **Levine, Molly.** 1992. "The Use and Abuse of *Black Athena*," *American Historical Review* 97.2 (1992): 440–60. **Lloyd, G. E. R.** 1991. "The Debt of Greek Philosophy and Science to the Ancient Near East," in *Methods and Problems in Greek Science.* Cambridge: Cambridge University Press: 281–98. **Loprieno, Antonio.** 1997. "Slaves," in Donadoni 1997: 185–219. **Martel, Erich.** 1996. "What's Wrong with the Portland Baseline Essays?," in J. Miller, ed., *Alternatives to Afrocentrism,* Ed. 2. Washington, D.C.: Center for the New American Community, pp. 30–34. **Merskey, Harold and Paul Potter.** 1989. "The Womb Lay Still in Ancient Egypt," *British Journal of Psychiatry* 154: 751–53. **Ortiz de Montellano, Bernard.** 1996. "Afrocentric Pseudoscience: The Miseducation of African Americans," in Gross-Levitt-Lewis 1996: 561–72. **Parkinson, R. B.** editor and translator. 1997. *The Tale of Sinuhe and Other Ancient Egyptian Poems 1940–1640 B.C.* Oxford: Clarendon Press. **Roth, Ann Macy.** "Building Bridges to Afrocentrism," in Gross-Levitt-Lewis 1996: 313–26. **Rutherford, Richard B.** 1995. *The Art of Plato.* London: Duckworth. **Vidler, Anthony.** 1987. *The Writing of the Walls.* Princeton: Princeton Architectural Press. **von Staden, Heinrich.** 1989. *Herophilus: The Art of Medicine in Early Alexandria.* Cambridge: Cambridge University Press; 1992. "Women and Dirt," *Helios* 19.1–2, 7–30. **Watkins, Calvert.** 1995. *How to Kill a Dragon: Aspects of Indo-European Poetics.* New York: Oxford University Press. **Wiedemann, Alfred.** 1883. *Sammlung Altägyptischer Wörter.* Leipzig: J.A. Barth.

GREEKS INVADING
THE ROMAN GOVERNMENT

Sir Ronald Syme

I

PEACEFUL INVASIONS achieve notable conquests. The Roman acquaintance with Greek civilization went back a long way. It was broadened and deepened when in the second century B.C. the imperial Republic defeated and broke the kingdoms founded by the generals of Alexander. Rome emerged as the dominant power in the world—all in the space of fifty-three years, as the historian Polybius was insistent to proclaim. Diverse and fateful perspectives opened.

One of them, not under discussion by Romans at the time, was the survival of their language. A conquering people is not always able to preserve it. Think of the helpless Normans, who lost their language in France and for a second time in England.

Latin, it is clear, was saved by two potent factors. First, that hard, crude speech had already been shaped and refined, on Greek models, to produce drama and a national epic (prose among this prosaic people took much longer to develop). Second, the Roman performance in law and government, achieved under the guidance of an aristocracy both liberal and cohesive, had nothing to learn from the republics of old Hellas—and the new kingdoms had been shown inadequate.

The debt in civilization incurred by the Romans could never be denied, only qualified. A specimen will afford instruction. Cicero, in the preface to his *Tusculan Discourses*, conceded the Greek precellence in arts and science. But Romans hold the first place for law and civic life, for government and warfare, for religion and the family. And the national character: what *gravitas*, what *constantia*!

37

That was not all. The native genius could improve on the Greeks whenever Romans found it worthwhile to take pains. Cicero (one assumes) had oratory in mind, with a personal motive. He was familiar with the unobtrusive technique to which Plutarch devoted a treatise, namely how to practice self-laudation without arousing dislike. It shows percipience here and there, but ought to be superfluous for the educated class in most ages.

Plutarch dedicated the piece to a Spartan nobleman who vaunted an ancient (and legendary) pedigree, being the thirty-first in descent from Castor and Pollux, the brothers of Helen. This person (Julius Herculamus), so it happens to be known, was a Roman senator.

History has moved a long way. That the language and letters of Hellas might enjoy a renaissance in the efflux of time was not beyond hope, not even beyond a rational forecast. Greeks in the Roman governing class, however—that notion would evoke horror and incredulity from Cicero, and from many others in a long sequel.

II

Under the rule of the imperial Republic, the Greek lands had endured manifold disasters and tribulations, to mention only the constant drain of wealth to Italy. The matter can be illustrated by brief recourse to the balance of trade, to what are called "invisible exports." Italy sent out governors and soldiers, financiers and tax-gatherers, and Italy drew benefit in return, with enhanced prosperity (though not for all classes of the population). Those exports, be it added, were all too visible throughout the Eastern countries: legionnaires, rapacious bankers, and the governor parading in the purple mantle of war, preceded by lictors who bore axes on their rods. The earliest Greek term for the mandatory who carries the *imperium* is "a six-ax man" (hexapelekys). To the imperial people, by contrast, the emblems of power convey beauty as well as terror: in the phrase of the poet Lucretius, *pulchros fasces saevasque secures.*

Worse followed during the civil wars of the Romans, involving the whole world. A sequence of great "imperatores" arose, continuous from Pompeius to Caesar, to Caesar's heir and to Marcus Antonius: by a suitable term the Greek historian Appian styled them "monarchic party-leaders." From historical perspective the epoch returned to the kingdoms of Alexander's succession—as was apparent even to an author of modest pretensions such as Cornelius Nepos. The rivalries of the dynasts led to campaigns and battles east of the Adriatic; and the Greek cities paid the bill, with enormous exactions.

III

In the thirties came a certain respite and new prospects. When the cause of the Republic went down at Philippi, Marcus Antonius took for himself the better portion, the eastern lands; and two years later concord seemed to be established between the rival leaders when Antonius married the sister of Octavian. That alliance was celebrated by a poem that many have found enigmatic, the *Fourth Eclogue* of Virgil. It can be interpreted without effort as an epithalamium, the Golden Age being inaugurated by a son who will rule the world.

The child arrived, but it turned out to be a girl. The respite was brief. In 32 B.C. the young master of the Roman West picked a quarrel with Antonius and forced war.

The person and character of Marcus Antonius encouraged defamation, and he came to an unhappy end. His governing of the East has commonly been denied due recognition. Yet his aims were clear enough: to conciliate opinion and offer some compensation for Roman oppression and arrogance. His prime concern lay with the city aristocracies who held power and influence: magistrates and priests and ambassadors, orators and philosophers, artists and doctors. These men could usefully be enlisted in administration. For example, Antonius assigned the island of Cos to a grammarian, the city of Tarsus to the author of an epic poem. Further, as ruler of the vassal kingdom of Pontus he installed Polemo, the son of a famous orator from western Asia.

In fact, the new ordering accorded to the oriental dominions was firm and sagacious. In a wide sweep from the border of Egypt to the Black Sea five princes protected the eastern frontier and occupied much of the interior of Anatolia. In consequence, less territory under direct rule than at any time since the conquests made by Pompeius Magnus. The eastward extension of annexations had been one of the causes for the breakdown of the Republic.

An oriental empire was thus in process of formation. It corresponded with the facts of history, language, and civilization. And notably with geography, or with geopolitics—to use a term questionably popular about fifty years ago, but not to be disdained. The western boundary was the sea that separates Greece from Italy. Indeed, for long ages of history the Adriatic was to delimit empires and civilizations.

By land the Romans hitherto controlled only a narrow strip along the coast. Then as now, tangled and precipitous mountains forbade easy communication.

To overcome that impediment was an urgent task, perhaps conceived at the end by Caesar the Dictator. Caesar Augustus accomplished it, the principal and lasting achievement of his reign. Wars of conquest in Illyricum and the Balkans advanced the frontier to the Danube and won the land route from Italy to Byzantium, binding West and East together in a compact imperial structure.

If geography spoke for division, human will annulled it. Without the resources of the East, Italy was condemned to impoverishment and dishonor.

Under the name of Italy, now deemed united and in unison (*tota Italia*) the young Caesar organized a plebiscite, mustering patriotic sentiment for war and for the reconquest of the Roman dominion from a foreign enemy. It is not easy to refrain from quoting the version of Virgil. Antonius, the Roman clad in un-Roman armor (*variis Antonius armis*), with all the resources of the Orient behind him, marching from the lands of morning and the crimson ocean, *victor ab Aurorae populis et litore rubro*, while follows in his train (wicked, wicked), the Queen of Egypt: *sequiturque, nefas, Aegyptia conuinx.*

IV

The portrayal is moving and magnificent, yet in one point defective. The War of Actium was ambiguous in motive, conduct, and consequences. The poet put emotional emphasis on an Italian nationalism that was now taken to embrace Rome, by a novel definition: *hinc Augustus agens Italos in proelia Caesar*. Virgil omitted the loyal support of the Roman West, the broad frontier extending all the way to furthest Spain. I mean "frontier" in the American sense. That is, a prosperous and dynamic region, in course of rapid development. It included northern Italy, that is Italia Transpadana, until now part of a Roman province (Cisalpine Gaul), but had a long extension westward to France and Spain. In later terms of European history, the frontier may be defined as Venetia and Lombardy, Provence and Languedoc, Catalonia and Andalusia.

The new Romans of the western lands were mixed in origin; the old Italian emigration, the military colonists, and the natives of the better sort. All responded alike to the Caesarian cause and to an imperial patriotism. As a result, their progress accelerated.

So far the victors in a Roman war. What was to be the fate of the vanquished?

Rancor and emotion abated. There was no thought of penalty or revenge. Normal relations resumed. One sign is a great rush of intellectuals to the capital. In the forefront we observe Strabo, of a good family from Amaseia in Pontus, who went on to produce compilations of history and geography, and Dionysios of Halicarnassus. Dionysios moved on from the study of oratory to compose the annals of the Roman People, from its earliest origins.

Eloquent Greeks are now prominent in the Roman schools of rhetoric; and poets were not slow to eulogize patrons among Roman nobles or women and youths in the imperial family, the *domus regnatrix* as it might already have been designated. In short, Rome at once became the capital of the Hellenic literary world.

For the recaptured dominions in the East, few changes save in the matter of Egypt. Caesar Augustus refused to hand over the rich land of the Nile to the mercies of proconsuls or bankers. He segregated Egypt. He ruled there as a monarch, in the line of the Ptolemies, as their dynasty had succeeded the pharaohs.

For the rest, Augustus was happy to take over the vassal princes chosen by his failed rival. The fact is plain. Augustus inherited the *clientela* of Antonius, just as Caesar had acquired the adherents of Pompeius Magnus. And in like fashion, the city aristocracies. The educated class would find suitable employment in service to the monarch. Philosophers were not only teachers or counsellors in the precincts of power. Augustus put the Stoic Athenodorus in charge of the turbulent city of Tarsus.

V

As past history indicated and promised, the role of the Greeks in the dual empire seemed clear and compelling.

In the vision vouchsafed to Aeneas in the lower world, government of the nations proclaims the Roman: *tu regere imperio populos, Romane, memento*. Others, *alii*, may keep the primacy in arts and sciences. They will shape marble or bronze, they will scan and delimit the motions of the stars. They may also have the advantage in eloquence; *orabunt causas melius*. That verdict, one notes in passing, would have shocked Cicero, and it annoyed those who inherited or exploited renown.

The dynasty founded by Caesar Augustus went on to exhibit marked favor toward Hellenic civilization. Tiberius Caesar, not generally recognized as a philhellene, had a predilection for the poets of Alexandria. He reflected the taste of an earlier generation; he turned his back on the new classic writers of the Augustan prime. Moreover, the next rulers (Caligula, Claudius, and Nero) had in their veins the blood of Marcus Antonius, being descended from his daughters. With Nero the fashion for all things Greek rose to a notorious culmination.

In the twelfth year of his reign, Nero at last visited Hellas. Towards the end of the tour, before a grand concourse at the Isthmus of Corinth, he proclaimed the liberation of Greece from Roman rule. A text survives. As Nero declared in conclusion, he would have wished to bestow a benefaction on Hellas in her great epoch. But the Hellenes had been enslaved either by foreigners or by members of their own nation. What he now grants, however, issues not from compassion but from benevolence, and as a thanksgiving to the gods of Hellas, vigilant to protect their worshipper by land and sea. Others in the past had given freedom to cities, only Nero to a whole province.

VI

This document excites due attention and furnishes some entertainment. For present purposes the philhellenism of emperors will introduce a large topic: the relations between authorship and society, between education and government. Greek writers have been already noted in Augustan Rome, but there appears to be a dearth in the sequel, the benefits of peace and prosperity being slow to take effect. The first exponents of note are Dio (from Prusa, in Bithynia) and Plutarch. They were close coevals, born in the early years of Claudius Caesar. Their most productive epoch falls towards the end of the century.

Dio and Plutarch may be regarded as precursors of the Hellenic renaissance that comes to full flowering in the time of Hadrian. The term "precursor" is normally held suspect in studies of history or literature. It implies a future not known, and seldom to be predicted. The precursor may be only a predecessor, like Plutarch to Suetonius in the art of biography.

Nevertheless, the term has a pertinent application in this context. Both authors indulged in activities that, while congenial to their own natures, could not fail to win approbation from the Roman government. Brief allusion must suffice. Dio, a wealthy man himself, was at pains to alleviate the constant strife between the rich and the poor. He gave benefactions to his own townsfolk, and sermons of earnest exhortation. He told a riotous mob that they had no excuse, that poverty is the parent of good behavior.

Dio was urgent to extol the advantages of social harmony during his travels elsewhere, notably at Tarsus where the guild of linen workers was a cause of disturbances. Further, confronted with the rivalry of neighbor cities, he enjoined moderation and concord.

At Rome, Dio delivered orations in praise of monarchy. The king (so he explained) is called by Providence to his exalted estate: like Heracles he passes his life in toil and duty, he loves the citizens and the soldiers, and he selects only the wise and the good for his agents and counsellors.

All of which came as no surprise to the Emperor Trajan and to the audience. Plutarch, not so vocal, confined his advice to the ruling class in the cities. In his *Precepts of Government* he issued sharp admonition. They must cease from strife and ambition, forget the glories of a distant past, and abide in contentment under the superior power. Furthermore, the rule of Rome (he reminded them) was not a product of chance or violence. Virtue and Fortune had collaborated.

The signal contribution that Plutarch made was less obtrusive. He hit upon a genial device, the sequence of parallel biographies, from legendary heroes down to generals and statesmen. The two nations were thereby recognized as standing on parity.

VII

The next testimony follows in the reign of Hadrian, rapid and convincing. A mass of orators emerged in high publicity, giving their name to the "Age of the Sophists."

Meanwhile, the literature of the Latins went into decline. The period initiated by Seneca and Lucan terminated with Tacitus and Juvenal. Most of the writers derived from the provinces of the West. Moreover, political success ran parallel with the literary movement. The newcomers won influence, they captured strategic positions in government, and they ended by installing an emperor in the person of Trajan.

Under the dynasty now making its inception, the literary benefit accrued by paradox to the Greeks. At the capital the new Romans from the provinces followed a Greek line of education: hence continuity between Nero and Hadrian. It had been enhanced under the second dynasty, notably by Domitian.

VIII

Hadrian, more a Greek than a Roman, paid honor and deference to the exponents of Hellenic eloquence. On short statement, these men were the social and intellectual elite of the Greek world, which they adorned and dominated. Diverse regions contributed, in the forefront the cities of western Asia, with Polemo on early prominence, a descendant of the Polemo whom Antonius appointed ruler of Pontus. Old Hellas was less on show, but Athens, long dormant, was awakening to the role of a university city. Herodes Atticus soon equalled and surpassed the fame of the great Polemo.

Even without support from birth and wealth, the sophists were elevated by professional pride and by the applause of admiring audiences. Other ages may be disposed to less friendly appreciations. Polemo was ostentatious and arrogant. More is known about Herodes, and much to his discredit—a millionaire, proud, cruel, and vengeful.

In their products the sophists were verbose and often vacuous, yet not without utility to the central government. In the year 143, in the presence of Hadrian's successor, Aelius Aristides delivered an imperial panegyric. It is one world now, he proclaimed, a federation of cities under the presidency of Rome; and the only distinction that obtains is between Hellenes and barbarians.

The oration of Aristides has evoked sympathetic response from inquirers in the modern time. On another estimate it is a farrago of commonplaces, it contributes little to the understanding—and its credit may now be on the wane. Abundant evidence has accumulated about society and government, and a new fabric of history can be elaborated. It depends on facts and names seldom or never disclosed by the written record. Aristides (it is a disturbing thought) may have conceived an ambition to enter the Roman Senate. The year of his oration was opened by Atticus as *consul ordinarius*. The best that Latin eloquence could put up in this season was the African, Cornelius Fronto (from Cirta, in Numidia).

He was only a suffest consul, sharing the honor with half a dozen other senators.

I am now brought at last to confront the central theme: Greeks standing high in the Roman state. It was not a novel and recent phenomenon, and the feature that deserves emphasis is consuls from the Greek lands arriving much earlier than the great resurgence of Hellenic culture. The process will arouse curiosity and provoke comparison with other examples of the convergence between education and government.

IX

Senators from the Greek East. The topic embraces various components and it calls for careful distinctions.

First, the colonists. A *colonia* of Roman citizens is a portion of the Populus Romanus, wherever it be situated. Caesar, the Triumvirs and Augustus had planted a number of colonies for veterans from their legions in the lands beyond the Adriatic, to a total of close to twenty; from Macedonia to the shore of Pontus and the Syrian coast. Conspicuous among them were Philippi, Alexandria in the Troad, Berytus in Syria. Even the heart of Anatolia had a cluster of colonies, the principal being Pisidian Antioch.

It was no surprise that before long military colonies should provide officers for the army, financial agents of the Caesars, and then senators and consuls. (The earliest of their consuls come up under the second dynasty, one from Alexandria, the other from Pisidian Antioch.)

Second, products of the great Italian diaspora during the epoch of the imperial Republic. Like Spain, the East offered various sources of enrichment, and, unlike Spain, the appeal of a high culture as well as a life of leisure. Bankers and businessmen settled in western Asia, and, acquiring property, duly improved their condition.

Not all of the immigrants endeared themselves to the natives. One recalls the pogrom that ensued when Mithridates of Pontus invaded the Roman province of Asia. That episode was conveniently covered up in an era of peace and concord. Italians became valued members of society and might intermarry with local families of ancient repute, which would not impair their chances if they aspired to senatorial rank. Several specimens of the returned emigrant can be put on show at quite an early date.

Third, senators of indigenous origin. They fall into two classes, at first sight distinct. First, the descendants of princes whose kingdoms had been mediatized; before that, interlocked in complicated family alliances and producing highly variegated pedigrees. Second, the urban aristocracies. The contrast turns out to be imperfect. For example, the Celtic tetrarchs in Galatia formed close attachments to Pergamum.

For advancement at Rome the stronger claims and the brighter prospects would appertain to the Roman colonists, so it might appear. Not so, the facts refute. The western provinces present a curious and engaging parallel. In the south of France (Narbonensis, the old *provincia nostra*) the colonists could not compete with the descendants of native chieftains who acquired their citizenship from proconsuls of the Republic. Narbonne and Arles are outstripped by Nimes and Vienne, which had once been tribal capitals.

In the eastern lands, rank, honor and fame accrue to the descendants of dynastic houses. They make the firmest impact on the governing class. That is a noteworthy phenomenon. How then can it be known and established?

X

The evidence of contemporary writers refutes this. Pliny in his correspondence published an ample survey of life at Rome. Letters are addressed to eminent senators, but none to any of the prominent eastern magnates. Arguments from silence are often a dubious recourse. In this instance, silence affords various instruction. A whole group may be all but absent. No letter of Pliny notices Hadrian (consul in 108), or certain other persons in the nexus that was to produce the Antonine dynasty, such as Aurelius Fulvus (the future Antoninus Pius), or Annius Verus, the grandfather of Marcus Aurelius. The picture of Roman society is incomplete. It has to be supplemented from other sources.

Next, Juvenal. The wealth and pretensions of the eastern oligarchs was a theme to sharpen satire and embellish declamation. Juvenal kept off it. He reserved easy ridicule for lower specimens of the Greek invasion, denouncing the *Graeculus esuriens*; by the same token, silence about any prosperous and vulnerable newcomers from Spain and Narbonensis.

Finally, Plutarch. If anybody, Plutarch should have testified, in felicitous profusion. Inspection contradicts.

A passage in one of his treatises (*De tranquillitate animi*) deplores ambition pushed to morbid excess, and refers in passing to the behavior of certain Greeks. They make a moan because they are not senators, and, if becoming senators, because they do not achieve promotion to the highest rank. That is all. No individual in the voluminous writings of Plutarch is defined as both a Greek and a senator. Into one of his dialogues, set in Athens, enters a character labelled "the magnificent King Philopappus." Of whom, more later.

Enough has been said, and more than enough, to undermine faith in the written sources. One turns aside and looks for facts and names. Epigraphy is the guide and master, introducing a long and complex chapter in the annals of society and governments.

XI

In the year 1837, W. J. Hamilton (the Secretary of the London Geological Society) was travelling through the interior of Turkey. At Ankara this excellent epigraphist copied two inscriptions on the citadel (one of them by use of a telescope). Those documents disclosed the career of C. Julius Severus, who had been admitted to the Senate by Hadrian. He was styled a descendant of kings and tetrarchs, and further, "the foremost of the Hellenes."

For a long time the discovery attracted little attention. Classical scholarship was engaged with other and traditional preoccupations; the eastern provinces were slow to awaken the curiosity of historians; and the careers of senators had not yet come to be properly studied and compared.

Encouragement emerged from the German excavations at Pergamum and Ephesus in the eighties and nineties. They revealed the monuments erected by the magnates, their benefactions to the cities, and the men themselves, not known before, unless as bare names on lists of Roman consuls, such as Julius Celsus and Julius Quadratus (consuls late in the reign of Domitian).

Then Ankara came out with the full and desired information about Julius Severus. By singular felicity it fell to Mommsen to expound the document in 1901, almost the last of his contributions to history and epigraphy.

The lineage of Julius Severus was now declared, the ancestors being King Deiotarus, also two tetrarchs of the Galatians, and Attalus the King of Asia. More important, his kinsmen, Severus was cousin to four men of consular rank (Julius Quadratus, King Alexander, Julius Aquila, Claudius

Severus) and further, cousin to a large number of senators. About the four consulars (consuls under Trajan between 105 and 112), quite a lot could be said. I refrain.

The revelation should have inspired a comprehensive study of the eastern aristocracies. The results would have affected much of what the nineteenth century believed about imperial history. The lesson was there, but it took some time to digest.

Hesitations were abolished by an inscription from Pergamum published in 1932—and, by the way, not well published by the first editor, Wilhelm Weber. It revealed what could never have been suspected. The senator in question was another Julius Quadratus, namely C. Julius Quadratus Bassus of regal ancestry. After his consulship (in 105), he commanded an army corps in Trajan's second war against the Dacians. In the sequel Bassus governed three military provinces in succession, Cappadocia, Syria, Dacia; and in Dacia he died on campaign in the winter of 117.

XII

A man of Pergamum leading the armies of the Roman People only four generations after the vaunted victory of the West at Actium, that was beyond hope or fear or forecast. A rapid evolution had taken place. To explain that, it is necessary to revert to Nero.

In the cosmopolitan entourage of the Caesars, Greeks had acquired influence and important functions. At the beginning of Nero's reign the viceroy of Egypt is Claudius Balbillus, whose son married a daughter of the King of Commagene; and at the end, Julius Alexander, a renegade Jew, the nephew of the learned Philo.

A process was taking shape. Under what kind of rhythm and how far it might go, remained to be seen. Emperors might modify it, but they could hardly bring it to a stop. An autocrat is not omnipotent. There are facts he cannot fight against, groups and pressures he cannot resist.

Deliberate policy was not much in evidence. On the contrary, chance dominated, with a sequence of accidents that enforced acceleration. The stages may be set forth as follows:

(1) The fall of Nero. His philhellenic tastes and attitudes were premature, provoking annoyance among conservative Romans, and he further alienated influential groups in the upper order. But it was evil counsels and plain folly that subverted a dynasty that had struck deep roots of

loyalty in the duration of a century. If Nero, instead of parading at festivals in Greece, had chosen to visit the armies of the Rhine, he might have gone on in iniquity for a long spell.

The catastrophe unloosed civil war throughout the world; pretenders perished in turn; and the power went to a low-born Italian.

(2) The accession of Vespasian. While conducting the war in rebellious Judaea, Vespasian was proclaimed emperor through a military conspiracy managed by his chief allies, the Prefect of Egypt and the governor of Syria. Partisans got their rewards. Both now, and a few years later, a number were promoted to senatorial rank. As the historian Tacitus observes, some excellent men who rose high, others with success as their only virtue.

Of officers in the army, a conspicuous name is Julius Celsus, from Sardis, serving as tribune in an Egyptian legion. Nor were civilian agents neglected, the magnates who influenced public opinion in cities of western Asia. Julius Quadratus of Pergamum became a senator of praetorian rank. Another of these personages was Julius Candidus (his city has not been ascertained or the early stages in his advancement). For two of the three (Celsus and Quadratus) inscriptions supply in full detail the posts they held at Rome and abroad.

However, caution must intervene. These entrants were not numerous, and the phenomenon might not have been attended with rapid or momentous consequences.

(3) The new dynasty. The East declared an emperor, but the main benefit went to the West. It took a double form. Promotion followed for many adherents, and imperial patriotism or prejudices won reassurance. Nonetheless, there is no warrant for speaking of a period of reaction now to set in.

When the elder son of Vespasian succeeded to the throne, the world was happy. Titus is described as *amor et deliciae generis humani*. Favorites of the Roman people tended to die young. Titus passed away after a reign of two years and two months. Radiant prospects of the Greeks were not impaired by his brother, Domitian. As with Titus, education counted heavily in his favor, and accident intervened to accelerate the processes of history.

(4) The return of Nero. In the East the name of Nero kept a potent appeal. His sudden eclipse inspired a widespread belief that he was not dead but had escaped and would come back. A sequence of impostors

arose. In the propitious season of the eruption of Vesuvius a false Nero mustered supporters in Asia, marched to the river Euphrates, and found a welcome from the Parthian monarch.

The vivid language of an oracle announced that "the exiled man of Rome would return, raising a mighty sword and crossing the Euphrates with a myriad host." In fact, a decade later, while Domitian faced grave emergencies on the northern frontiers, Nero came up again. This time he received strong support from Parthia: not an aggressive power, it is true, but alert to exploit Roman embarrassments.

It was expedient for Domitian to overcome the memory of Nero and conciliate opinion in the eastern lands. A counter-measure can be divined. In the year 89 Domitian appointed Julius Celsus and Julius Quadratus as governors of imperial provinces in Asia Minor (Cilicia and Lycia-Pamphylia). In the routine of promotions, those posts normally led to consulships, and Celsus and Quadratus duly took office (in 92 and 94), Consulates for easterners, that had not been contemplated by Vespasian, or by others, when they entered the Senate twenty years previously.

There is something else for the rubric. The enigmatic Julius Candidus (who had meanwhile become consul in 86) was now put in charge of Cappadocia, the great military command that faced Armenia.

(5) The accession of Trajan. Nero passed into the realm of legend and myth and apocalyptic visions, but he might come back in another incarnation. The Emperor Titus, so some opined at Rome, might turn out to be a second Nero: not for the better reasons, and the satirist Juvenal called Domitian a bald-headed Nero. According to one estimate, Nero returns in the person of Hadrian.

We are waiting for Hadrian. Trajan is interposed, a more decisive factor in the present theme. After the assassination of Domitian in 96 the government of Nerva soon ran into trouble, and a veiled coup d'état imposed one of the army commanders, M. Ulpius Traianus, the governor of Upper Germany. Trajan, by ultimate origin Italian, came from the far edge of the western world (Italica, near Seville). His main support rested upon a nexus of alliances in the new imperial nobility from Spain and Narbonensis.

Rome now had a ruler, an *imperator*, whose claim and whose facade was military and traditional—of primary import, but not intended to deceive. There was another aspect. Trajan in youth had come to know the eastern provinces under his father, legate of Syria and proconsul of

Asia. Results become apparent early in the reign. In the year 100 he consigned the Syrian command to his Pergamene friend, Julius Quadratus, although he had never seen an army hitherto.

The choice declares one of the open secrets of the imperial system. Usurpers themselves, the Caesars had reason to distrust birth or talent. Personal loyalty was paramount, age or mediocrity no bar.

The next manifestation was more startling. On return from Syria, Quadratus opened the year 105 as consul for the second time. His colleague in the *fasces* was Julius Candidus. Second consulates fell to few, save close allies of the Emperor.

The crown of a senator's career was to govern either Asia or Africa (Celsus and Quadratus duly acceded to Asia). There was one post of higher dignity, the city Prefecture, reserved for the most eminent—and indeed for very few, the tenure often being for life. Julius Candidus became *praefectus urbi*, probably in 105. Inferred by some scholars from the second consulship, the fact has only recently come to knowledge. It is certified by the inscription of one of his descendants found at Ephesus.

In 105 warfare resumed on the Danube. As has already been indicated, the other Pergamene notable, Julius Quadratus Bassus (consul suffect in that year), led an army in the conquest of Dacia and went on to be governor of three military provinces.

Names and facts have been adduced that are absent from the memorials of written history—and some not yet accorded due recognition in modern narrations. Eastern consuls are no longer to be regarded as sudden or sporadic products. All in all, during the two decades of Trajan's reign, a total of about twenty can be identified. In the forefront stand the magnates, with kings and tetrarchs for ancestors, as disclosed by the inscription of Julius Severus at Ancyra. For the rest, a variegated company, with only two from old Greece (one of them the parent of Herodes Atticus). The process that took its inception under the second dynasty has developed into an invasion of the governing class. The newcomers appear firmly ensconced in the new imperial nobility, the oligarchy of the consular families.

As concerns the Imperator himself, ambition was not satisfied by renewing ancient military glory and extending the Empire beyond the Danube. He insisted on settling accounts with the Parthians. The enterprise conveyed a powerful appeal to the Greek world, and a further impulsion towards partnership in empire. Rome took up an old quarrel, revenge on the Persian and the Mede—and Trajan was susceptible to the praises of Alexander the Macedonian.

XIII

The war failed, and Trajan's successor had to cover up a debacle. Greeks continued to exploit the blessings of peace under manifold encouragements. Hadrian's policy and predilections were amply advertised at the time, and they do not fail to earn eager approbation.

All that is known and conceded. The present discourse proceeds on a narrower front. It concentrates on the personnel of government.

The reign of Hadrian opened under evil auspices. In the first year four of the marshals of Trajan met their end for treason, on charges of conspiracy that cannot have been easy to render convincing. Hadrian had sore need of friends and allies in the upper order, notably the army commanders with whom the arbitrament resides in a season of crisis.

The record is sadly imperfect. Nonetheless, during the twenty-one years of his reign, only two Greeks were put in charge of consular armies. As one looks to the list of consuls in sharp contrast to the *annus mirabilis* under Trajan, at the most one Greek lends his name to the Roman year as *consul ordinarius*.

What consequences should be drawn? That is a question. In the first place, no setback in the general advance of the Greeks. After the influx under Trajan accidents of age and of demography may have caused an apparent abatement, and some of the first consuls left no male issue. Still, one might wonder.

Of set purpose the present enquiry plays down the role of individual emperors, putting emphasis on forces beyond their control; yet personality cannot be excluded. Hadrian was complex and capricious; and a ruler may be inclined to build up a contrast between himself and his predecessor. His character both attracts and repels. The history, such as it is, cannot furnish an adequate answer, nor can fiction help very much, despite the *Mémoires d'Hadrien* of Marguerite Yourcenar (1951). The book receives well-merited acclaim: it is a masterpiece of classical and archaic prose. Yet, as Edward Gibbon said of the poetry of Claudian, it fails to satisfy or to silence our reason. The author has taken over sundry items from a variegated and often doubtful source, the notorious *Historia Augusta*.

A proper and cautious estimate indicates that Hadrian was averse to pomp and national pride, hostile to the claims of birth and wealth and class. On reliable information, his favorite philosophers were Epictetus and Heliodorus. The former, a severe moral teacher, had been born in slavery, the latter (of lesser fame) belonged to the Epicurean persuasion.

A suspicion arises: Hadrian failed to respond to Trajan's enthusiasm for the descendants of kings and tetrarchs. If so, his preference went to the more modest type, to the cultivated urban aristocracy.

XIV

Hadrian selected for his successor a senator endowed with a character contrary to his own, the steady and tranquil man known as Antoninus Pius. The family came from southern France (from Nîmes), but had become, like others, metropolitan in tastes and habits long since. Pius was the third consul in his line.

No changes were to be expected from Pius, and no disadvantages for Greeks. The consulship of Herodes Atticus in 143 is accorded prominence perhaps too much and too often. Another Athenian and a Pergamene were the consuls of the previous year.

The Emperor himself, it is true, was not enamored of talkers and thinkers. His ironical language, published in an edict, offers a hint of how he might judge the aristocracy of the intellect. The Roman government granted various exemptions and privileges to teachers and doctors and others. But, said the Emperor, a philosopher will not claim financial benefit that would show him not a genuine philosopher.

Education and money and the name of Herodes Atticus raise a sharp question. What was the use and value of eastern senators?

XV

At Rome the *novus homo* had to work his way. He rose to public honors through the service of the state. At the same time, social eminence continued to assert its prerogative, alike among survivors of old families and among the recently ennobled. Their function was largely decorative, with no need of enhancement through military or civilian merit. Some of the eastern magnates conformed to this class.

While Trajan was on campaign beyond the Euphrates, the city of Athens witnessed the construction of the huge mausoleum that stands to this day on the Hill of the Muses. It commemorates Philopappus, the grandson of the last ruler of Commagene, with for ancestors the Seleucid monarchs of Syria. While bearing the title of King, Philopappus was also (as one of the inscriptions states) a Roman senator, by his full style C. Julius Antiochus Philopappus, admitted to the high assembly by Trajan, and a consul (in 109).

The curious will also note (and marvel) that King Philopappus was a member of the Arval Brethren, that primeval fraternity that had been revived (and all but invented) by Caesar Augustus. Apart from lavish banquets, the Brethren, convened to reiterate ancient rituals or celebrate dynastic occasions, which might supply a suitable pastime in a life of dignified leisure—if Philopappus ever attended the meetings. It is not likely that he was often seen in the Senate, although it harbored a mass of mediocrities worthy of most of the business there transacted.

At home in Roman society through the community of education and habits, eastern senators had not been fully integrated, like their counterparts from the western provinces. They tended to go back. In the course of time ex-consuls may be discovered superintending the construction of buildings or in long sojourns at temples and health resorts.

The illustrious Philopappus had no occupations in provinces or armies. When his Athenian monument was erected, the memory of a better man found honor at Ephesus. The heirs of Julius Celsus built a great library at Ephesus (the city he preferred to his native Sardis). When the visitor begins to ascend the steps at the entrance he can contemplate on either side the inscribed record, the Latin version facing the Greek. He there reads about the career of Julius Celsus, from military tribune in Egypt to the Asian proconsulate.

The Library of Celsus stands as solid testimony to the alliance between education and government, made manifest towards the end of Trajan's reign. Before long that alliance comes out in fine style, in the career and writings of Arrian. Steady productivity in a long life carried a wide range of interests, including history, not only Alexander and the successors but the Roman wars with the Parthians.

The author is known and valued. Less attention has gone to the senator and consul. Born at Nicomedia in Bithynia, Valves Arrianus as a young man attended the lectures of the philosopher Epictetus (he wrote up and published his notes many years later). The early stages of his career evade ascertainment. He served as an officer in Trajan's war and entered the Senate soon after, so it might be conjectured. The command of a legion should be assumed; and he was probably proconsul in the far West, governing the province Baetica (the home land of Trajan and Hadrian), as an inscription found at Corduba renders plausible. Then, consul in 129 or 130, Arrianus went on to hold the military province of Cappadocia for six years (double the normal tenure). His reports to Hadrian are extant.

Hadrian and Arrian were congenial in many tastes: not only Epictetus but cavalry maneuvers. And both liked horses and dogs.

Cursory reference has been made to the admired masters of eloquence —such as Herodes Atticus and Aelius Aristides, not without allusion to deleterious features in the Hellenic renaissance. A man like Arrian helps to redeem the Age of the Sophists.

XVI

In his oration Aristides declared that there are no wars any more, merely trivial unrest among border tribes. Warfare now belongs to myth or memory. Concord and stability prevailed—or, in other words, a firm alliance of the propertied classes east and west. Thus passed the twenty-three years of Antoninus Pius in deep calm, or in a mild torpor that seemed beneficent.

When Pius died in March of the year 161, he transmitted a secure government to Marcus Aurelius, the nephew of his wife, the husband of his daughter. The other adoptive son of Pius was Lucius Verus. Marcus promptly associated him as equal in power. Moreover, Marcus, deemed by the Roman highly suitable for a ruler, was now, like Titus, completing his fortieth year. And, by an abnormal felicity, five months later Faustina presented him with twin sons—one not long surviving, the other named Commodus.

During long ages the wise and the good had scarcely dared to hope for a philosopher on the throne. He was now vouchsafed by Providence. But Fortuna holds dominion over the nations, and Fortuna turned against, with no delay or hesitance.

Calamities followed without cessation. The Parthians inflicted defeats on two Roman armies, and when the victorious legions returned four years later they brought with them the plague. Then Germans and Sarmatians came over the Danube, hence long years taken up with continuous campaigns, and Marcus himself at the head of the armies for most of the time.

Epochs of disturbance throw up great generals and may imperil the reigning dynasty. Should Marcus perish, a Greek regent was not out of the question.

In 169 Lucius Verus died. His widow Lucilla was transferred to Claudius Pompeianus, a military man of low birth from Antioch in Syria. Another daughter of Marcus had married Claudius Severus, an eastern aristocrat (grandson of a cousin of Julius Severus). Marcus much admired Severus: he was expert in the philosophy of Aristotle.

Severus and Pompeianus had the rare distinction of a shared consulate in 173. If in concord, they might have carried on the government and protected the dynasty.

XVII

Two years later Avidius Cassius proclaimed himself emperor in Syria. Cassius had won great glory in the Parthian War, and stayed on as governor, soon invested with a superior *imperium* over the Eastern provinces. In short, vice-gerent for Marcus, and for many years. Like Domitius Corbulo under Nero, Cassius became *capax imperii.*

Cassius was equipped with other advantages. He was the son of Heliodorus, the Epicurean philosopher, friend and secretary of Hadrian and appointed Prefect of Egypt in the last year of the reign. Heliodorus came from northern Syria and perhaps asserted kinship with the regal house of Commagene. An Avidius Antiochus happens to be on record.

The proclamation of Avidius Cassius caused (and continues to cause) surprise and consternation. Old Herodes Atticus, so it is alleged, sent him a missive in a single Greek word: "You have gone off your head."

Other explanations avail: an accident and a mistake. One turns to the historian Cassius Dio, who at that time was about twelve years old and not incapable of recalling what they said about this transaction. Dio supplies two statements. First, the deteriorating health of Marcus alarmed his consort. In fear of his death Faustina wrote to Cassius. She urged him to be in readiness, and she offered him her hand. Second, rumor reported the decease of Marcus, and so Cassius made his abortive proclamation.

Scandal and detraction hangs over the memory of Faustina, perpetuated in classic and eloquent form by Gibbon: "the grave simplicity of the philosopher was ill calculated to engage her wanton levity," and so on (taken from the *Historia Augusta*).

Dismissing the tradition about Faustina, a sober estimate arises without discomfort from the political situation in the spring of 175. Providing against an emergency, a sagacious and resolute woman took action to preserve the succession for the boy Commodus (now age thirteen) and safeguard her own position by annexing a powerful ally as regent.

The pair may have been old acquaintances, congenial and even close in age. A piece of papyrus can be adduced. It is identified as Cassius' announcement to the citizens of Alexandria. He styles Alexandria his native city. That term may yield the date of his birth. In 130 Hadrian visited Egypt. If his parent Heliodorus was imperial secretary at this time (and nothing forbids), he accompanied Hadrian, as had Suetonius on the journey to Britain. On this hypothesis the youthful prime of age would be added to the other advantages of the pretender.

XVIII

Epilogue. The Greeks in their ascension thus came out with a potential emperor of high capacity. Champions of Hellenism fell by the way, such as Antonius and Nero, but the process had gone on, not to be abated by any form of resistance. It is a story of accidents, of opportunism, and of political success. Above all, the success of higher education: a topic not to be disdained in an exposition presented to a university audience.

What the writers tell us is shown inadequate on so many counts. The other testimony (that is, epigraphy) is likewise sporadic and fragmentary. To become intelligible, history has to aspire to the coherence of fiction, while eschewing most of its methods. There is no choice, no escape.

In the present discourse I have conveyed the reader on a long promenade through the centuries by devious paths and not without digressions; the way led through a dense forest of facts and names, a veritable *selva selvaggia*.

Voltaire somewhere says that facts are vermin that infest history and prevent understanding. Another feature may be found even more repellent. The perpetual expansion of the governing class at Rome is nothing but the annals of the few and the fortunate.

The concept of elite, like the word itself, enjoys a certain disfavor in the modern time. Historical scholarship takes to embracing the laboring poor with eager solicitude or with doctrinaire affection. Not to much profit or exhilaration, at least as concerns the study of antiquity. Peasants and slaves did not speak or write, their condition denied them freedom

of action. By good fortune, the Hellenes, although not always in possession of the liberty that they cherish even to excess, exhibit and avow a
strong tendency to be active, visible, and vocal.

PART TWO

The Byzantine World

THE DIVINE EAST-ROMAN EMPIRE

Joseph Gill, S.J.

WHEN DID the Byzantine Empire begin? Some historians would say in 330 when Constantinople was founded; others favor 476 because it marked the end of the Western Empire; still others urge 717 with the advent to the eastern throne of Leo the Isaurian. E. Barker (with most other modern historians) affirms that the arguments in favor of the earliest of these dates are "conclusive not only because the foundation of Constantinople proved to be the centre and brain that was to inspire the Empire of the East for over a thousand years, but also (and this is the greater reason) because the foundation of Constantinople was synchronous with the acceptance of Christianity as the basis and core of the Empire, and because the essence and heart of the Byzantine Empire, from first to last, was the Christian faith which invested the Emperor with his "god-founded" power and determined the nature of the community over which he ruled."[1]

Norman H. Baynes described that nature in these words: "The basis of the political philosophy [of the Christian Empire] is to be found in the conception of the imperial government as a terrestrial copy of the rule of God in heaven: there is one God and one divine law, therefore there must be on earth one ruler and a single law."[2]

Even before the advent of Christianity Providence had so guided the evolution of the pagan Roman Empire under its "divine" emperors that its world domination, its admirable administrative organization and road system, and especially its *pax romana* made possible the rapid diffusion of the faith of Christ. When the Emperor was Constantine, Christian at heart even if not yet baptized, the Roman Empire became also the Christian Empire, the counterpart of the kingdom of heaven. "All authority is from God"; and all authority on earth resides in the Emperor, who "is

exalted over all worldly things, the representative of Christ; who unites
in himself the whole fullness of all earthly power and who, therefore,
bears also the immense responsibility for the maintenance of peace and
justice, for the preservation and expansion of the Empire, for the repres-
sion of barbarians and for the safeguarding of the unity of the faith."[3] The
Emperor was head of both Church and State, for, as there was one
Empire, so there could be but one head. Church and State were not two
things but one, the arena in which the great Christian drama of the
Redemption would be worked out until it reached its completion in the
next world. It was a religious faith. "It appeals not to philosophical
systems or theories, but in the first place to a faith, which binds together
the after life with this, the spiritual with the temporal, in a grandiose
vision stemming from a unified point of view."[4] "That was, in spite of its
grandeur, so simple a concept that it could not help being understood
even by the last peasant in the most remote corner of the Empire, and the
last *stratiotes* was ready to pour out his blood for it."[5]

     This ideology, then, was a combination of *romanitas* and *christian-
itas*. The pagan Roman Emperor had already been the wielder of all
authority in the state, *pontifex maximus*, custodian of the *ius publicum*,
and indeed usually deified at least after his death. Constantine, elect of
God, was all these with modifications. He retained the title, *pontifex
maximus*, but he was not a priest. Yet, as custodian of law and responsible for order, he was entitled to control the religious activity, if not the
faith, of all his subjects, Christians as well as pagans, especially if it
menaced the unity of the State. That he soon did when he arranged for
local synods to deal with the Donatists and particularly when he
summoned the Council of Nicaea—and the bishops did not protest.[6] He
could not be adored as a god but he could be reverenced as God's vice-
gerent.

     Both East and West shared this fundamental ideology, but historical
events broke the political unity and caused different developments in
different areas. In the West, shattered by wave after wave of invasion,
romanitas, after much travail, emerged as a loyalty to the Church of
Rome: in the East, undisturbed by invasion, it remained as a loyalty to the
Emperor as the heir of Constantine, the Roman Emperor, and to the
Empire of the Romans of which he was the head.

     The choice of those who filled the imperial throne was directed by
divine Providence, employing the traditional machinery of the old

Roman Empire—the votes of army, senate, and people—so that the elect could be accounted the *deputatus* of God. "It is God, not I, who confers this dignity on you," said Emperor Justin II to Tiberius, when he created him Caesar, and at a coronation the people's acclamation (a traditional formula of words) was: "Glory to God who has appointed you as Emperor, who has glorified you and shown you his grace." A certain Niculitzas, writing shortly after 1080, probably to Alexius Comnenos, declared: "God has raised you, our revered Lord, to the throne of kingship and made you by His grace, as you are called, a terrestrial god, to do and act as you wish; therefore let your acts and deeds be full of understanding and truth, and let justice be in your breast."[7]

Hence, the Emperor was habitually and officially called "divine" (*theios*), "holy" (*hagios*), "God-crowned" (*theosteptos*). When Patriarch Joseph I in 1281 in a letter omitted "hagios" from the Emperor's titles, Michael VIII saw in it a threat of *lèse majesté* and immediately demanded an explanation.[8] All ceremonial coins, seals, even garments had "an underlying symbolic meaning—the mystical glorification of the Emperor."[9] Coins were struck with the Emperor's effigy on one side; perhaps with the crown being placed on his head by celestial hands, and on the other the effigy of Christ. He wore the richest of rich robes and they were often changed. He alone could wear purple shoes. When he wished to be seen by the people, he had to stand on rich carpets or polished porphyry. In the sessions of the council of union in Ferrara (1438) he insisted on a special door being made near his throne, so that he could be carried unseen through a series of empty rooms to his place.[10] He alone signed his name in cinnabar—red ink. In his presence all remained standing and in silence, even princes: he spoke in monosyllables and through an intermediary. His throne was wide enough for two, because he shared it with Christ. On Sundays and feast days he sat at the left end, leaving the right for Christ; on ordinary days he conducted his court as Christ's vice-gerent and sat in Christ's place on the right.[11] It was a privilege not granted to all to offer proskynesis to the Emperor, but no proskynesis to him was allowed on Sundays so as not to seem to rival God. All this and a host of other practices were designed to impress that he was different from other mortals, a personage apart, the next in dignity to God Himself.

The ceremonial at his public audience was shattering. Liutprand described his experiences in the Magnaura Palace.

Before the emperor's seat stood a tree, made of bronze gilded over, whose branches were filled with birds of every kind also made of gilded bronze, which uttered different cries, each according to its various species. The throne itself was so marvelously-fashioned that at one moment it seemed a low structure, and at another it rose high into the air. It was of immense size and was guarded by lions, made either of bronze or of wood covered over with gold, which beat the ground with their tails and gave a dreadful roar with open mouth and quivering tongue. Leaning upon the shoulders of two eunuchs I was brought into the Emperor's presence. When, at my approach the lions began to roar and the birds to cry out, I was neither terrified nor surprised, for I had previously made enquiry about all these things from people who were well acquainted with them. So after I had three times made obeisance to the Emperor with my face upon the ground, I lifted up my head, and behold! the man whom just before I had seen seated on a moderately elevated seat had now changed his raiment and was sitting in the level of the ceiling. How it was done I could not imagine, unless he was lifted up by some sort of device as we use for the raising of the timbers of a wine press. On that occasion he did not address me personally, since even if he had wished to do so, the wide distance between us would have rendered conversation unseemly, but by the intermediary of a secretary he enquired about Berengar's doings and asked after his health. I made a fitting reply and then, at a nod from the interpreter, left his presence and retired to my lodging.[12]

The majesty of the pagan emperors had been acknowledged by their apotheosis after death and their images were worshipped even during their lifetimes. The Christian emperor deserved no less. St. Gregory Nazienzen in his *Adversus Iulianum* wrote: "Neither their crowns and diadems and bright purple nor the number of their bodyguard nor the multitude of their subjects is sufficient to establish their sovereignty (*basileia*); but they need also adoration (proskynesis) in order to seem more sublime, adoration directed not only to them personally, but also that made to their images and portraits, in order that a greater and more perfect honor be rendered to them."[13] So, in St. Gregory's day and long after, as many as entered the imperial presence prostrated themselves till their foreheads touched the ground. Later, to offer such proskynesis was the privilege of only the highest dignitaries. The kissing of the knee, the cheek, the mouth—all or some of these were what was accorded to lower dignitaries according to their rank. Michael VIII by the treaty of 1261 showed his special favor to the city of Genoa by granting its *podesta*, the honor of offering proskynesis, when the Venetians and the Franks were allowed only a simple genuflection.

From 457 onwards after his election by the army and the senate the Emperor was crowned by the Patriarch, whereby God seemed through the Church to be solemnly confirming the choice of his faithful servant, and the Emperor was given a quasisacerdotal status within the Church. Hence he could do things that simple laymen could not do. He was the *deputatus* of God; he could enter the sanctuary during the Holy Liturgy; he could communicate himself from the consecrated chalice, incense the altar, give the blessing to the congregation, kiss the altar linen, the paten, the relics; he could read the gospel at solemn services and preach.

It was not unusual in Byzantium for laymen to debate theology. Emperors did it also, but with more authority, and their activities in that field could have momentous consequences. Iconoclasm (whatever its root-causes, about which there are various theories) would not have torn Byzantium apart and caused many martyrdoms if the Emperors Constantine VI and Leo IV, father and son, had not espoused it with a kind of religious fanaticism, nor would it have been checked if Empress Eirene had not had a like passion for the traditional practices. In the fourteenth century John VI Cantacuzenus supported Gregory Palamas in his theological defense of Hesychasm. After Cantacuzenus had been crowned in Constantinople in 1347 till the end of the century, the patriarchs of Constantinople and all new bishops of the Greek Church were Palamists, opposition was stamped out by persecution, and the prestige of the Church grew both at home and in other countries of oriental rite. When Manuel II Palaeologus was in France in 1401 seeking help in men and money to save his capital and Empire seemingly in its last throes, besieged as it was by the Turks, he was questioned on the *Filoque* doctrine. His answer was a book of one hundred and fifty-six chapters.

Nevertheless Emperors were not priests and could not perform purely priestly functions. Their state, however, was in a way elevated above that of priests and was equiparated with that of bishops. Balsamon (c. 1140–c. 1195), Patriarch of Antioch and celebrated commentator on the Church's law, wrote: "For as Emperors are said to be, and are, anointed of God, so bishops are and are said to be. This is shown also from the fact that the prayers recited when Emperors are crowned and when bishops are consecrated have the same power.... And note that both the imposition of hands in the case of bishops and the anointing in the case of Emperors wipe away sins committed before the consecration and the anointing, whatever they are."[14] Another famous commentator, Demetrius Chomatianus, who after Theodore Doucas had captured Thessalonica in 1224 and crowned him emperor, wrote as follows: "In a word, with the sole exception of sacred functions, the Emperor luminously exhibited the other high-priestly prerogatives, provided he acts legally and canonically.... Since an Emperor is also the Christ of God because of the chrism of imperial sovereignty, but Christ, our God, is among other things High Priest and as such is proclaimed, so with good grounds is also he, the Emperor, adorned with the high-priestly charism."[15]

These, to our minds, exaggerated exaltations of the imperial status and prerogatives were not just the fantasy of the simple and uneducated layman fascinated by the pageantry of imperial symbolism. It was part and parcel of the philosophy of empire that was accepted without question by all the citizens of the Eastern Empire, both high and low, lay and ecclesiastical. The bishops did not challenge Michael VIII's assertion (13 January 1261) that "the Emperor is subject neither to laws nor canons," or that, in spite of the ancient canon that forbade the transfer of a bishop from one diocese to another, the Emperor could "remove even metropolitans from their metropolies, divide up their territories, create new bishoprics, direct bishops to function in dioceses not their own."[16] It was the Emperor who had the last word in the appointment of the Patriarch of Constantinople. They synod proposed three names from which he selected one or, if he favored none of them, he nominated someone else whom the synod automatically accepted. He then presented him with the symbols of office, saying, "The favor of God and of Our sovereignty that flows from it promote this most pious person to be Patriarch of Constantinople."

In the eyes of the people the Emperor was the first after God. He was raised to a height as near to the throne of God as any creature could possibly be. In prayers connected with the Holy Liturgy—the most solemn of all religious acts of praise and worship of God performed by the Church—his name is closely associated with the Three Persons of the Blessed Trinity. Prayers for the feast of Pentecost are an example.

> Oh N. and N., crowned of God, the most high Trinity discloses itself unreservedly well-pleased with your crowning, for on this day the Father gives the Tables to Moses, the Son bestows the Spirit on the disciples, the Spirit himself appears in the form of tongues of fire. Your feast

is threefold. Today the consubstantial Trinity that crowns you is professed.

> The Spirit who is God today was manifested to the Apostles in the form of tongues of fire, and you, crowned benefactors, has he honoured with the purple and the crown, and rightly by his divine will has he judged that you rule the Romans worthily. Glory to God who has crowned you to the honour of the Romans.[17]

The whole situation has been effectively summarized.

> By elevating a man above the ordinary faithful, by recognizing in him the elect of Providence but at the same time the servant of God, the champion of orthodoxy, the Church rendered his authority sacrosanct. Every insult, every plot, every violence, even involuntary, against his person became a sacrilege deserving death; every revolt against his authority involved excommunication, and rejection of the faith and rebellion against the Emperor were branded with the same name of apostasy. It is this political and juridical aspect of the imperial religion that explains its longevity.[18]

It was in the nature of things that the Emperor should make the laws and that their enforcement should depend on him and his subordinates.

He was not only lawgiver, he was the law—in Justinian's phrase he was the "nomos empsychos," the living law. He personified the law. He made the law both in the political sphere and in the ecclesiastical sphere. Normally the bishops enacted canons in their synods and the Emperor imposed their observance by adding the sanction of the law of the state. Sometimes, indeed, even in respect of the faith, Emperors took the initiative, as when Zeno in 482 and Heraclius in 638 proposed dogmatic formulae, which the eastern bishops obediently accepted but which the western Church rejected. In the West an Emperor was not above the law but subject to it. St. Ambrose of Milan warned Emperor Theodosius to do penance for his sin before attempting to enter his church and refused an imperial edict to hand over to Arians a Catholic temple. But even bishops like Ambrose and popes like Leo I and (in the time of Zeno) Felix III did not challenge imperial power except in the context of faith. Pope Gelasius (492–96), while vindicating to the Church the *auctoritas* of the popes, willingly recognized the *potestas* of the Emperors, though he denied them *sacerdotium*. For the great lawgiver of Byzantium, Justinian, "The priesthood and *imperium* do not differ so very much, nor are sacred things so very different from those of public and common interest" (decree of May 535).[19] But as Dvornik concluded after a long study of Justinian, the lawgiver: "Justinian understood the *imperialis potestas*—with all the implications given it by Roman lay—as placing the spiritual sphere under its care for the normal functioning of the *sacerdotalis auctoritas*. Unlike the popes, he limited the functions of the *sacerdotium* to intercession on behalf of the imperium."[20] So both were encompassed in his famous codex of law that legislated as much for the Church as for the State: the Church did not repudiate the claim. Towards the end of the twelfth century Balsamon, commentator on church law, wrote: "The service of the Emperors includes the enlightening and strengthening both of soul and body; the dignity of the patriarchs is limited to the benefit of souls and to that only."[21]

This was the attitude of the East until the Iconoclastic Controversy (726), when the people and the monks, supported by the Church of Rome, stubbornly resisted the Emperors' attacks on images and finally, but only after nearly a century of fierce contention and persecution, prevailed. But that did not produce any serious modification of the Emperor-image. So, even though after the Iconoclastic Controversy relations between Church and Emperor were never quite the same, their basis, the unique position of the divine Emperor as representative of God to guide the Empire of the Romans to its spiritual destiny of salvation, remained unshaken. He was the law. Leo the Wise (886–912), less than fifty years after the end of Iconoclasm, justified his abolition of certain traditional powers of the state in the process of lawmaking with these words: "Today everything depends on the wisdom of the Emperor, and all things are supervised and managed, with aid from heaven, by the providential care of his wisdom."[22]

Byzantium, however, received a shock in the year 800, when in Rome Pope Leo III crowned Charlemagne, king of the Franks, as emperor. That was not because the West had repudiated the philosophy of empire current in the East. It was because the East could not match its philosophy with practical acts of worldly politics. It could not defend the pope and the Church in Italy against the Lombards, who had overrun the Byzantine exarchate in Italy and in 751 had taken its administrative center, the city of Ravenna. Constantinople was grievously affronted and ignored the new emperor till the need to secure its Illyrican frontiers by a treaty with the new western power made it concede the title "Emperor" to Charlemagne (812). But thereafter, to show the universality of their empire as against the limitations of a local potentate, the Byzantine emperors more frequently added "of the Romans" to their title to indicate that they alone were the successors of Constantine the Great, Emperors therefore of the Roman Empire that he had bequeathed and of all its subjects, who alone could rightly be called Romans. When Charlemagne's empire broke up after his death, his successors were addressed only as "kings."

The belief that the Byzantine Empire was the continuation of the Roman Empire remained in eastern minds unshaken and unshakable till the end. When in 968 Liutprand, bishop of Cremona, went with a letter of Pope John XIII recommending "his beloved and spiritual son Otto, august Emperor of the Romans" to "Nicephorus, the Emperor of the Greeks," the western envoys were thrown into prison at the insult. "The Greeks abused the sea, cursed the waves.... The audacity of it," they cried, "to call the universal Emperor of the Romans, the one and only Nicephorus, the great, the august, 'Emperor of the Greeks', and to style a poor barbaric creature 'Emperor of the Romans'."[23]

In 1352, when the Eastern Empire was being battered by Turks, Venetians, and Genoese, it was still the Empire of the Romans. Patriarch Philotheus, after the pillage of Heraclea by the Genoese, wrote:

> And the situation now is such that those of the New Rome, that is, all of us who belong to the universal Church and are subjects of the Roman Empire and therefore continue to call ourselves Romans, differ so greatly from those of the Old Rome and all the various principalities of that now divided nation that very few of them recognize the fact that they too were once Romans and of the same nation and Empire and that the cause of their present detachment from the Church as from the Empire is their own short-sightedness and folly.[24]

Forty years later, when the political situation was even worse and Constantinople, besieged by the Turkish Sultan Bayezid, was in imminent danger of capture, Patriarch Antonym admonished the Prince of Moscow, who had stopped the commemoration of the Byzantine Emperors in the Liturgy: "It is not possible for Christians to have the Church and not to have the Empire. For Church and Empire have a great unity and community, nor is it possible for them to be separated from one another." "The holy Emperor is not as other rulers and governors.... He alone is the lord and master of the oikoumene."[25]

The name "Roman" was a legacy of history, not a factual indication of race. "All the countries that had once belonged to the Roman *orbis* and later joined the Christian Church were considered by the Byzantine Emperor as their everlasting and incontestable possessions."[26] Together they formed the Roman Empire. "A Roman, therefore, is that citizen of the sole legitimate Roman Empire of Constantinople who at one and the same time professes the correct faith of this Empire, orthodoxy, and is a member of the world's one divinely ordained community, the predominantly Greek- and Christian-oriented community of the East-Roman Empire."[27] So, as Goths, Vandals, Avars, Slavs, Armenians, and many more settled in Byzantine territory, all became *Romaioi*, subjects of the God-given Emperor who ruled the world in God's name.

As the years went by, in practice not all Christians recognized Byzantine suzerainty. After A.D. 800 the whole of the West went its own way. Nearer at hand, Bulgars and others set up kingdoms of their own. But Byzantium never admitted facts that contradicted ideas: it devised face-saving formulae. If it made a treaty, it was not a mutually agreed arrangement, but a concession granted by the Emperor: till 1261 not both parties signed a document but only the Emperor and that in the form of a chrysobull logos, the formula used by the Byzantine court for granting powers and privileges. If Byzantium was forced to pay tribute to a dangerous tribe, it was described as a "gift" to the peoples concerned in recognition of their help in guarding the frontiers. If independent rule of some prince had to be accepted, it was never suggested that it was gained by force but it was "conferred" by the Byzantine Emperor, who alone had full power. The Emperor was always ready to be godfather to kings being baptized into the Christian Church. In 864 Boris of Bulgaria was baptized Boris Michael, adopting the name of his godfather Emperor Michael III. Henceforward he was the Emperor's spiritual son. Byzantine diplomacy created out of the surrounding states and tribes an imperial "family," of which the Emperor was the "father." According to their size or importance of the needs of the moment, heads of such states were sons, or brothers, or friends, or even servants, titles that implied respect and a certain dependence on the Basileus. All embassies brought gifts, which the Byzantines chose to regard as signs of subservience. The presents that the Emperor gave in return—seals, brooches, plaques—often bore his effigy, which, if worn or displayed, diffused an impression of humble loyalty offered to the imperial throne.

Such devices combined with the splendor of the Byzantine ceremonial that surrounded the Emperor and the magnificence and pageantry of the eastern Holy Liturgy in the Church of St. Sophia were not ineffectual in promoting wonder and a feeling of inferiority in many of the Empire's neighbors. But they could not disguise the fact that after the year 800 the Western world was independent. It was, perhaps, inevitable that the founding of a New Rome would lead to rivalry. It came soon and at first it was ecclesiastical.

When Constantine established his capital in Byzantium, he meant to set up a replica of the organization of Rome in his new city, where the language spoken would be Latin. Constantinople was to be another Rome. Inevitably, ecclesiastically it could not remain the humble suffragan of Heraclea that it had been. It became a metropolitanate and, as church organization tended to develop *pari passu* with civil administration, since it was the chief city of the Eastern Empire, so its church grew in stature. Hitherto rank in the ecclesiastical world had been influenced by two factors, foundation by an apostle and the political importance of the place. Rome could appeal to both titles. It had been founded by St. Peter, the head of all the apostles, and it enshrined not only his tomb but also that of St. Paul. It was, too, the capital of the Empire. Alexandria ranked second: it claimed to have been founded by St. Mark, St. Peter's evangelist, and unquestionably it was at the head of all the flourishing Christianity of Egypt. The rapid growth in importance of the Church of Constantinople decreed that the Bishop of Constantinople should have "primacy of honor after the Bishop of Rome on account of the city being the new Rome." In the contest between Alexandria and Constantinople Alexandria lost, and after the Council of Chalcedon monophysite Egypt was in schism.[28]

That council repeated and developed the Constantipolitan claim. According to the so-called Canon 28:

> we decide and vote about the primacy of the most holy church of the same Constantinople, new Rome. For indeed to the throne of the elder Rome, on account of that city being the seat of government (*to basileuein*), the Fathers rightly conceded the primacy. Moved by the same consideration the 158 God-beloved bishops allotted to the bishop of new Rome equal primacy, having with reason judged that the city which has been honored as the seat of government (*basileia*) and of the senate, which also enjoys equal primacy with the elder imperial Rome, should be held in high repute like it.[29]

Pope St. Leo I informed both the Emperor and the Archbishop of Constantinople that he did not recognize the canon. But history was against him. The Western Empire declined in importance under barbarian invasions; the Eastern continued to flourish and the Church of Constantinople, despite papal disapproval, did in practice enjoy a primacy.

Pope Leo had based his rejection of Canon 28 on two grounds, the claim that the headship of the Church given by Christ to St. Peter continued in Peter's successors, the bishops of Rome, and the rejection of the statement that the ecclesiastical rank of either Rome or Constantinople depended on the political accident of imperial residence.[30] From now on the West was committed to the Petrine theory and the East to (what one might call) the political theory. The rivalry between the Churches of Rome and Constantinople had started. It was destined to continue, the conscious or unconscious basis of all the frictions from then till now, the most divisive of the many divisive factors that, as time went on, bred schism and maintained it.

The words "New Rome" in the decrees of the years 381 and 451 by mistake or design gave a wrong nuance of meaning. Emperor Constantine intended Constantinople to be a second Rome, the first remaining undiminished, but "New Rome" implies a replacement by a livelier, pulsating capital of an old and dying city. So there arose a theory of "renovation" and the belief that Constantinople transplanted lock, stock, and barrel the organization of government and the senate to the new site, leaving nothing in the old.[31] Pope Nicholas I seems to attribute such views to Photius.[32] They are very forcibly expressed by an outraged patrician eunuch of the court of Nicephorus II Phocas to an intimidated Liutprand: "The silly blockhead of a pope does not know that the sacred Constantine transferred to this city the imperial sceptre, the senate and all the Roman knighthood, and left in Rome nothing but vile slaves, fishermen, confectioners, poulterers, bastards, plebeians, underlings."[33] Anna Comnena had no doubt about it: "For when the sceptre and the senate and simultaneously the entire officialdom were transferred from there [Rome] to this place, to our land, to our imperial city, the archiepiscopal rank [of the ecclesiastical sees] was also transferred and the kings of those days gave the primacy to the throne of Constantinople and in particular the Council of Chalcedon, having elevated [the see of Constantinople] to the first rank arranged under this all the dioceses throughout the world."[34] The idea was still alive in the middle of the fourteenth century. In 1354 Demetrius Cydones consulted "those in power" about his proposed adoption of the Latin faith. His advisers, to dissuade him from pursuing his purpose, praised the site and the amenities of Constantinople and said that "in all such points the elder Rome was inferior and that he should, therefore, not attach himself to it nor should he still call it 'Rome', manifestly sunk, as it was, in decay from old age; but he should stick to the new, since it was at its peak, and should take it as his teacher in things divine, which were guaranteed by the judgements of the Emperors who resided there and of the four patriarchs who all agreed, to contradict whom was to wage war on God and the truth."[35]

Foundation by Constantine the Great and succession to him in the government of his Roman Empire were the cornerstones of the claims of Constantinople and its Emperors to pre-eminence. To steal their thunder, so F. Dölger suggests,[36] the West discovered the *Donati'o Constantini*, according to which Constantine the Great freely bestowed on Pope Silvester complete authority and jurisdiction in the West, leaving with him his own diadem with which he should crown western emperors. Such a *Donatio*-document was produced and its text is extant. But it was not the work of a pope nor was it originally directed to impress Constantinople. It was a forgery made in Rome, probably between 754 and 767, for local purposes.[37] It rapidly gained a wide credence in the West, where it was not challenged until the middle of the fifteenth century by Lorenzo Valla, who proved that it was spurious. For the controversialist, it provided a perfect answer to the eastern claims, since it made Constantine a quasi-founder of the Roman Church and of papal jurisdiction, and that before he did anything for Byzantium.

When the *Donatio* first came to the attention of the Greeks cannot be said, perhaps in the tenth century. Humbert of Moyenmoutier, the writer of Pope Leo XI's reply to Cerularius's attack on Roman practices, made much of it, quoting it at great length.[38] H. Ahrweiler believes that Constantine Porphyrogenitus knew of it and concluded from it that Rome's claims were ill-founded, since it could be argued from the *Donation* that Constantine in 330 founded not a second Rome, but the one and only Rome.[39] Certainly the Byzantine historian Kinnamos drew from it an argument against the primacy of Rome and the independence of the West. Their authority, he claimed, was a concession from the Emperor of Constantinople and so Rome and the rulers of the West were inferior. "They have reached such a pitch of audacity as to declare that the kingship in Byzantium is different from that of Rome"; the truth really was that all rulerships outside of Constantinople were derived "like particles from the imperial power."[40] The western schism was aggravated by heresy. It had refused to accept the twenty-eighth canon of Chalcedon, which was to spurn the decision of a general council.

The disasters that befell Byzantium in the last centuries of its existence did not destroy the faith of its inhabitants that they were the *Rhomaioi* ruled by a God-crowned Emperor, but it did make some thinking men wonder how long the Empire could survive. It was on the verge of collapse in the last decades of the twelfth century, which helps to explain why the Fourth Crusade could twice capture so strongly fortified a location. The loss of their Queen City forced them to face up to their situation, and it made them reflect on their past. Without renouncing their name *Rhomaioi*, they began to think of themselves as Hellenes, a title that over the centuries had denoted, not Greeks, but pagans, and that was never hitherto used for Byzantines. With a freshly awakened pride in their glorious ancestry of classical times, the defenders of Marathon, the sculptors, architects, poets, orators, and philosophers, they found a new pride and developed a new sense of nationhood. They regained Constantinople and much of their old Empire, but the incessant internal rebellions and civil wars, the inexorable advance of the Turks that, bleeding from their self-inflicted wounds, they had not the strength to check, and the stranglehold that the Italian mercantile states of Genoa and Venice established, led inevitably to their becoming vassals of the infidel and then the victims. To the end they were the *Rhomaioi* of God's Empire on earth.

NOTES

1. E. Barker, *Social and Political Thought in Byzantium* (Oxford, 1957), p. 27.

2. N. H. Baynes, "Eusebius and the Christian Empire," in *Byzantine Studies and Other Essays* (London, 1955), p. 168.

3. F. Dölger, "Die Kaiserurkunde der Byzantinen als Ausdruck ihrer politischen Anschauungen," in *Byzanz und die europäische Stattenwelt* (Ettal, 1953), p. 11.

4. *Ibid.*, p. 10.

5. F. Dölger, "Bulgarisches Zartum und byzantinisches Kaisertum," in *Byzanz*, p. 143.

6. Cf. W. Ullmann, "The Constitutional Significance of Constantine the Great's Settlement," in *Journal of Ecclesiastical History*, XXVII (1976), 1–16.

7. Quoted by Barker, *Social and Political Thought*, p. 126.

8. G. Pachymeres, *De Michaele Palaiologo*, ed. T. Bekker (CSHB) (Bonn, 1835), p. 506.

9. G. Ostrogorsky, "The Byzantine Empire and the Hierarchial World Order," in *Slavonic and East European Review*, XXXV (1956), 3.

10. *Les Mémoires de Sylvestre Syropoulos sur le Concile de Florence (1438–1439)*, Concilium Florentinum Documenta et Scriptores, vol. IX, ed. V. Laurent (Paris–Rome), p. 329.

11. O. Treitinger, *Die oströmische Kaiser—und Reischsidee nach ihrer Gestaltung im höfischen Zeremoniel vom oströmischen Staats—und Reichs gedanken* (Darmstadt, 1956), pp. 32-33.

12. *The Works of Liutprand of Cremona*, ed. F. A. Wright (London, 1930), p. 207.

13. *Adversus Julianum*, II PG 35 605, translated by F. Dvornik in *Early Christian and Byzantine Political Philosophy: Origins and Background*, II (Dumbarton Oaks, Washington, 1966), p. 666.

14. A. Michel, *Die Kaisermacht in der Ostkirche (843–1204)* (Darmstadt, 1959), p. 11.

15. *Ibid.*

16. *Collection of the Divine and Holy Canons*, ed. G. A. Rhalles and H. Potles, III (Athens, 1853), 349-50.

17. Constantine VII Porchyrogenitus, *Le Livre des Cérémonies*, ed. A. Vogt (Paris, 1935), II, 5.

18. L. Brehier, *Le Monde Byzantin*, II *Les Institutions de l'Empire Byzantin* (Paris, 1949), pp. 87–88.

19. Dvornik, *Early Christian and Byzantine Political Philosophy*, p. 816.

20. *Ibid.*, p. 817.

21. Barker, *Social and Political Thought*, p. 106.

22. *Ibid.*, p. 100.

23. Liutprand, *The Works of Liutprand of Cremona*, p. 263.

24. Quoted by D. M. Nichol in "The Byzantine View of Western Europe," in *Greek, Roman and Byzantine Studies*, VIII (1967), 324-35.

25. *Acta et diplomata graeca medii aevi*, II *Acta patriarchatus Constantinopolitani*, 1315-1402, ed., F. Miklosich and J. Muller (Vindobonae, 1862), pp. 194-96.

26. Ostrogorsky, "The Byzantine Empire and the Hierarchical World Order," p. 5.

27. F. Dölger, "Rom in der Gedankenwelt der Byzantiner," in *Byzanz*, p. 77.

28. N. H. Baynes, "Alexandria and Constantinople: A Study in Ecclesiastical Diplomacy," in *Byzantine Studies*, pp. 97–115.

29. *Conciliorum Oecumenicorum Decreta*, ed. Albergio, Ioannou, Leonardi, Prodi (Basel, 1962), pp. 75–76.

30. J. D. Mansi, *Sacrorum Conciliorum nova et amplissima collectio*, 6, 191B (letter to Emperor Marcian), and 206A (letter to Archbishop Anatolius).

31. The Roman senate remained in Rome and was active: "The pagan resistance [to the abolition of pagan sacrifices] was undoubtedly widespread, but its core in the West was the Roman senate, which, after Rome had ceased to be the capital of the Roman Empire, assumed once more in Roman history a conspicuous role" (H. Bloch, "The Pagan Revival in the West at the End of the Fourth Century," in *The Conflict between Paganism and Christianity in the Fourth Century*, ed. A. Momigliano [Oxford, 1963], p. 194).

32. Cf. F. Dvornik, *The Photian Schism* (Cambridge, 1948), p. 124.

33. *The Works of Liutprand*, p. 265.

34. Anna Comnena, *Alexias*, ed. B. G. Niebuhr (Bonn, 1839), CSHB, I, 13, p. 64.

35. D. Cydones, "Apologia for his Faith," in G. Mercati, *Notizie di Procoro e Demetrio Cidone*, Studi e Testi 56 (Città del Vaticano, 1931), p. 370. This was written c.1354, when Byzantium, exhausted by civil war and Turkish depredations and having lost Asia Minor to the Turks and half its European territory to the Serbs, was involved in the rivalries between Genoa and Venice. Whichever Italian city would win, Byzantium would still lose, and so sent embassies to Rome to beg for papal help.

36. F. Dölger, "Rom in der Gedankenwelt der Byzantiner," pp. 107ff.

37. R.-J. Loenertz, "Constitutum Constantini: Destination, Destinataires, Auteur, Date," in *Aevum*, XLII (1974), 199–245; N. Huyghebaert, "La donation de Constantin ramenée a ses véritables dimensions," in *Revue d'Histoire Ecclésiastique*, LXXI (1976), 45–69; P. J. Alexander, "The Donation of Constantine," in *Mélange G. Ostrogorsky*, I (Receuil de Travaux Just. Byz. 8), pp. 11–25.

38. Cf. PL 143 751AB, 732BC, 753A–755D.

39. H. Ahrweiler, *L'Idéologie de l'empire Byzantin* (Paris, 1975), p. 49.

40. John Cinnamus, *Epitome rerum ab Ioanne et Alexio Comnenis gestarum*, ed. A. Meineke (Bonne, 1836), p. 219; *Deeds of John and Manuel Comnenus,* trans. C. M. Brand (New York, 1976), pp. 166–67.

GREECE AND BYZANTIUM

Donald M. Nicol

GREECE TODAY STANDS at the end of two powerful traditions: the Hellenic and the Byzantine; the ancient and the medieval. The two traditions have something in common. Both were evolved and conveyed in the Greek language. But the Byzantine tradition was Christian, the Hellenic was pagan; and the Byzantines were always a little suspicious of the legacy of ancient Greek literature and philosophy. To them a Hellene meant an unredeemed pagan. Definitions of periods of history are bound to be relative. The end of the Middle Ages in Europe is sometimes arbitrarily set in the fifteenth century, about the time of the discovery of America. But in Greece the Middle Ages, or the medieval period of the country's history, lasted well into the eighteenth century. The Byzantine Empire as a political institution had a beginning, a middle and an end. It began in A.D. 330 when Constantine founded his New Rome on the site of the ancient Byzantium and it ended on Tuesday 29 May 1453, when the Ottoman Turks conquered the city of Constantine. But its ideas and its spirit lived on among the Greek-speaking people for centuries after that date and their influence is still far from spent.

The soil of Greece today is littered with the ruins of classical antiquity. The most impressive of them are temples, for temples were built to last. Greece is also littered with the monuments of its Byzantine or medieval past. And here again, most of them are temples, or rather Christian churches. The many Byzantine churches and monasteries of Greece do not look as if they were built to last. Their masonry and brickwork sometimes appear slipshod and clumsy compared with the finesse of the ancient temples. But they have lasted because they have been in constant use ever since they were built. The monastery church of the Great Lavra on Mount Athos was built in 963, and though its dome has now and then collapsed, it has been in daily and nightly service as a Christian temple for 1020 years. It was built in the middle age of Byzantium. It continues to exist and to serve its divine purpose in the modern age of Greece. The legacy of ancient Greece to the whole world is so overwhelming that one can scarcely quantify it. The legacy of Byzantium was not so widely spread. But it has influenced all the European countries that once formed part of the Byzantine Empire and, most of all, Greece itself.

Its most obvious manifestation is the Orthodox Church. This is not surprising. In 1453 the Sultan Mehmed II, who had conquered Constantinople, needed a representative of the millions of Orthodox Christians within his empire. He picked the monk Gennadios. It was the Sultan who invested Gennadios as patriarch, handing him his insignia, his robes, his staff, and his pectoral cross, as the first Patriarch of Constantinople under the Muslim dispensation. Gennadios was given the task of working out a lasting concordat between triumphant Muslims and humiliated Christians. He was the Ethnarch, the leader of the Christian *millet* or nation within the Ottoman Empire. He and his successors were to be personally answerable to the Sultan for the conduct of that *millet*. It was a heavy responsibility. The Byzantine Church in all its long history had never been burdened with so large a measure of secular authority.[1]

Byzantine political theorists had generally held that church and empire, patriarch and emperor, went together. A church without an empire was an impossibility. The one could not exist without the other. In 1453 they were proved wrong. The empire as a political institution was dead. But the Church lived on as the embodiment of the Byzantine spirit and tradition. It is often said that the Orthodox Church kept the torch of Hellenism alive during the dark centuries of the Turkish occupation of Greece. This is a persistent myth. What the Church really kept alive was the Byzantine Christian tradition. Constantine Sathas, a great scholar and a great patriot of modern Greece, once described the Patriarch Gennadios as "the last Byzantine and the first Hellene."[2] Gennadios would have liked the tribute. "I do not call myself a Hellene," he said, "because I do not believe as the Hellenes believed. I might call myself a Byzantine because I was born at Byzantium. But I prefer simply to call myself a Christian."[3]

The surviving Byzantine Church quickly came round to the idea that the empire still existed, albeit in another form. Christians still lived under a theocracy. The emperor was now unfortunately a Muslim. But he was still the Basileus, the Sultan-Basileus, ordained by God to rule the world from Constantinople. Kritoboulos of Imbros, one of the historians of the fall of the city, dedicated his work to "the Supreme Autokrator, Emperor of Emperors, Mehmed... by the will of God invincible Lord of land and sea."[4] The Church nonetheless encouraged the hope of a miracle. Prophecies abounded, foretelling that the Christian Empire would be restored, however briefly, before the Second Coming of Christ and the end of the world. The priest who had been celebrating the Liturgy in Hagia Sophia on that fateful Tuesday had disappeared behind the wall of the sanctuary when the Turks broke into the cathedral. He would yet return to finish his interrupted sacrament.[5] There was a legendary king who had been turned to marble and lay asleep in a hidden cave near the Golden Gate of Constantinople. At any moment he would awake and expel the infidel from the city. His name was sometimes John and sometimes Constantine. But in either case, his waking would be heralded by the bellowing of an ox. All these hopes and fears were to be found in a huge corpus of messianic and prophetic literature, including the so-called Oracles of Leo the Wise. They were eventually assembled in a prophetic book ascribed to one Agathangelos, who was said to have lived in Sicily in the thirteenth century. In fact, the compilation was made by a Greek archimandrite from Adrianople in the eighteenth century. It was immensely popular and had a wide circulation in manuscript and printed editions.[6]

For at least two centuries after the fall of Constantinople this was the kind of literature that shaped the minds and the hopes of the Greeks. The Church and the Christian faith were for long their only links with the past and their only certainty for the future, whether in this world or the next. There is no evidence that the Greeks of these centuries felt any affinity with the Hellenes of antiquity or read any of their works. The Byzantine Church had, in any case, always taught that true wisdom could only come through grace and revelation; and what, said one of its saints in the fourteenth century, of these things could Euclid, Ptolemy, Socrates or Aristotle have known? "To know God in truth is immeasurably greater than all the philosophy of the Hellenes."[7] The Church was also suspicious of the new technology. It had to keep a watchful eye on what the Greek printing presses of Europe were publishing. The first such press in Constantinople was set up in 1627. The machinery was imported from London by that eccentric and enterprising Patriarch, Cyril Loukaris, sometimes called the "Protestant Patriarch." It seems never to have printed anything, for it was destroyed by a combined effort of the Janissaries and the Jesuits. The Turks thought it was a secret weapon. The Jesuits were jealous, because they had their own Greek press in Rome for churning out anti-Orthodox propaganda.[8]

Greek books were, of course, printed elsewhere in the Orthodox world in the seventeenth and eighteenth centuries, notably in Romania, in the principalities of Moldavia and Wallachia, and by the Greek community in Venice. But it was the Church that called the tune and paid the piper, or rather the printer, for what it considered to be fit reading matter for the Greek Christian public, whether within the Ottoman Empire or in the diaspora. The great majority of books printed were of a religious nature—liturgical texts, psalters, gospels and the like. This was so until the middle of the eighteenth century, when some Greek presses began to print translations of the authors of the new enlightenment in the West. The Church was quick to censure this tendency. But even in the eighteenth century, when some new ideas were beginning to filter through the ecclesiastical net to the Greek-reading public, religious works still held the field. Out of 1521 books printed between 1700 and 1800, 956 (or about 60%) were religious in content. The other 40% did not, as one might have hoped, include the works of Homer, Plato, or Aristotle. The secular literature most in demand was clearly not that written in classical Greek, unless one includes Aesop's fables, which ran through twenty printed editions between 1775 and 1821. The *Erotokritos*, for example, was reprinted seven times in the eighteenth century, and the *Romance of Alexander the Great* six times.[9]

It was towards the end of the eighteenth century that things began to change. Greek schools were founded at Ioannina, Chios, Smyrna, and other cities, where a feeling for the glorious past of ancient Greece was deliberately imparted. They were endowed by wealthy Greek businessmen, such as the Zosimades brothers of Ioannina, who had made their fortunes in the West and knew what the western world expected of the Greeks. It expected them to be Hellenes, the proud descendants of Pericles and Themistocles, not pitiable Byzantine Christians. Paintings of the "Hellenic philosophers," Plato, Solon, Aristotle, Plutarch, and Thucydides, had already appeared on the walls of churches in the sixteenth century. In the late eighteenth century they begin to appear no longer labelled as Hellenes and adorned with haloes, as Saint Ploutarchos and

Saint Thucydides.[10] But for the most part, people still felt more at home with the familiar forms and faces of their Christian saints than they did with these exotic creatures from their allegedly Hellenic past.

By then the Greek War of Independence was drawing near. Theodore Koloktronis, one of the heroes of that war, liked to wear what he thought was a Homeric helmet. That was about the extent of his classical education. He admitted that his childhood reading had been entirely religious—the prophecies of Agathangelos, the psalter, the *oktoechos* and the lives of saints.[11] Rigas Pheraios, who in 1796 drew up a Constitution for the as yet to be constituted "Hellenic Republic," had already persuaded a publisher in Vienna to print an edition of the prophecies of Agathangelos.[12] Rigas Pheraios, or Velestinlis, was one of the first to break out of the Byzantine mold, but only to a limited extent. The Constitution of his proposed Hellenic Republic, like the map that went with it, was designed to cover the inhabitants of Rumeli (or Turkey in Europe), Asia Minor, the Archipelago, and the Danubian principalities of Moldavia and Wallachia. All these people were said to be descended from the ancient Hellenes. The official language of this Republic was to be Greek; its citizens were to be known as Hellenes, not Romaioi. The revolutionary flag was to show the club of Hercules surmounted by three crosses. It is significant that the Church was left out of account. But in other respects what Rigas envisaged was a restored Byzantine Empire, with Constantinople as its capital.[13]

The most celebrated Neohellenist of this age was Adamantios Koraes. Koraes hated Byzantium and the Byzantine spirit and tradition, which he saw as a dead weight on the otherwise pure and free Greek spirit. His mission in life was to recall the Greeks to the great heritage of their ancient past. His most important work in this respect was his Hellenic Library (*Hellenike Bibliotheke*). This was a series of classical texts supplied with edifying introductions about the cultural, educational, and linguistic problems of contemporary Greece.[14] Koraes was a great man and a great scholar. But for most of his life he lived in western Europe. He was the son of a silk merchant in Smyrna and tried to go into business for himself in Amsterdam before settling in Paris. He was an absentee patriot, seventy-three years old when the war of independence broke out in Greece; he was deeply influenced by the enlightenment and the political ideas of the French Revolution. These were the ideas that fed the flames of the Greek desire for liberation, and for a national identity as Hellenes.

For Koraes, as Arnold Toynbee put it, "Modern Western Enlightenment" and "Classical Greek Hellenism" were interchangeable terms.[15]

Enlightened western Europeans of the early nineteenth century, captivated and brainwashed by Edward Gibbon's account of Byzantium, were inclined to blame the Greeks for their own degeneration under the Ottoman Empire. They should never have allowed themselves to sink into the superstition and decadence of that monk-ridden society. As Koraes would have agreed, it was the Byzantine period of their history that had promoted the corruption of the Greeks, which had merely been consummated by the Turks. What, as one German scholar put it, was the point of studying a depraved form of the Greek language in which the preposition *apo* takes the accusative instead of the genitive case.[16] Such were thought to be the symptoms of the Byzantine corruption of the soul and spirit of ancient Greece.

It would be unkind to say that the Orthodox Church had a vested interest in maintaining that state of corruption. But certainly the Church was alarmed by the winds of change blowing from the West in the eighteenth century. Its leaders condemned the baleful influence of the new enlightenment and French revolutionary thinking on the minds and political aspirations of their flocks. In 1768 at Leipzig, Eugenios Voulgaris published the first Greek translation of one of the works of Voltaire. Translations of Locke, Descartes, Newton, Rousseau, and others followed.[17] A Greek enlightenment seemed in danger of breaking out. The liberal principles of western European thought found eager audiences in all the cities where there were Greek communities—in Paris, Vienna, Budapest, Venice, Rome, Bucharest, Jassy, Odessa, Moscow, St. Petersburg, and in Constantinople itself. The Church and its aristocratic patrons reacted swiftly to this dangerous development.

By 1790, the patriarchate had its own printing press in Constantinople. Patriarchs, bishops, monks, and laymen poured out pamphlets that were widely distributed, denouncing, often in the most violent terms, the philosophers and scientists of the West. Voulgaris, translator of Voltaire, had by then been invited to the court of Catherine the Great in St. Petersburg. He changed his tune and became a bishop. In 1791 he published a tract called *In Refutation of a Certain Impious Prattler*. Two years later the "prattler," Voltaire, was officially condemned by the Patriarch of Constantinople—and along with him Rousseau and Spinoza. One of the pamphlets produced that same year is entitled: *The Wretchedness of the*

Pseudo-Sages, or an Apology on behalf of the Christian Faith towards the Refutation of Certain Philosophical Babblings. Another is called: *A Reply to the Irrational Zeal of the Philosophers Coming from Europe.*[18]

"The teachings of these new libertarians," as one of the patriarchs wrote, "are hostile to the Holy Scriptures and to the Apostolic teaching...and should be hated as a device of the fiendish Devil, ever alert for the spiritual destruction of Christians." In the 1790s the Patriarch of Constantinople issued a series of encyclicals warning the faithful against "the wily snares of unrest and rebellion" being propagated by the French.[19] In 1798 a document was published in the name of the Patriarch of Jerusalem called the *Paternal Exhortation (Didaskalia Patrike)*. It restated in unambiguous terms the old Byzantine theory of the divine order of things. The Ottoman Empire was the guardian of that order. It had been set up by God. The Sultan ruled by God's grace. The current western notions of political liberty were inspired by Satan.

> Our Lord raised out of nothing this mighty Empire of the Ottomans, in the place of our Roman Empire which had begun, in some ways, to deviate from the beliefs of the Orthodox faith; and He exalted the Ottoman Empire higher than any other kingdom so as to show without doubt that it came into being by divine will and not by the power of man, and to assure all the faithful that in this way he deigned to effect a great mystery, namely the salvation of His chosen people.[20]

The Church also mistrusted the revived interest in the ancient Greek heritage and in the natural sciences in Greek schools and colleges. Both represented "Hellenism" in the worst and pagan sense. By all means let young men study the writings of selected classical authors for style and grammar; but they must beware of their content. In the seventeenth and eighteenth centuries the models for style in writing Greek were still those that had been favored in the middle and late Byzantine era. Voulgaris translated his Voltaire into ancient Greek, not into the spoken language of his time. Alexander Mavrokordatos, who held the distinguished and lucrative post of Grand Interpreter to the Sublime Porte for close to forty years, wrote all his published works in the ancient language. Even his letters are in the highly rhetorical style of Byzantine epistolography; and indeed they were used in Greek schools as exemplars of the genre, along with the letters of Libanios and Synesios. Byzantium still ruled the rhetorical waves.

The Greek language was, of course, also a part of the Byzantine heritage, whether in its pure *katharevousa* form or in the demotic, vulgar version. The co-existence of "learned" and "popular" forms of Greek was, indeed, older than Constantinople. If it was true, as Koraes maintained, that "the character of a whole nation may be known from its language," then it was important to reach some agreement about the form of that language, for fear that you might end up with two nations instead of one. Koraes himself favored what might be called an evolutionary purifying of the spoken tongue.[21] Others of his day were for developing the demotic to the exclusion of the literary form. Still others were "Atticisers" pure and not so simple, who would have everyone talking and writing a dead language. Enthusiasm for the new Hellenism took some strange forms. In 1817, at the Greek college at Ayvalik (Kydonies) on the coast of Asia Minor, the excited students passed a resolution to converse only in the language of Demosthenes and Plato. "The gross and vulgar language," they resolved, "is wholly unbecoming to us as the descendants of the ancient Hellenes. Each of us, therefore, is to speak, so far as possible, in the Hellenic language. Whoever does not do so is, as a punishment, to recite a page of Homer before us."[22]

The students also resolved to change their names. They could no longer put up with Christian names such as Iannis, Georgios, and so on. They would adopt names worthy of their ancestry, like Xenophon, Aristides, or Themistocles. This practice, too, was quickly condemned by the Church. In 1819 the Patriarch Gregory V fulminated against what he called "the innovation of giving ancient Greek names to the baptized infants of the faithful." The Patriarch also warned the faithful against the perils of the natural sciences, which could lead only to ungodliness and atheism. He was all for education, but it should be confined to grammar, rhetoric, and true religion. "For what use is it," he asked "to the young to learn numbers and algebra, and cubes and cube roots, and triangles and triangulated tetragons...and elliptical projections, and atoms and vacuums, if, as a consequence, in speech they are barbarians, ungrammatical in their writings, ignorant of their religion, degenerate in their morals... and unworthy of their ancestral calling?"[23] The students at Ayvalik and the Patriarch Gregory were in agreement that young people should make themselves worthy of their ancestors. But they were thinking of different sets of ancestors.

Alexander Mavrokordatos was one of the Phanariote Greeks of Constantinople, those privileged and wealthy aristocrats who served the Sultan in various ways, especially as the princes of Moldavia and Wallachia in the eighteenth and nineteenth centuries. Their special relationship with the Turks did not make them traitors to Christianity. Their fortunes helped the Church to survive; and the world in which they made their fortunes was the world of Orthodox Christianity. It extended from Moscow in the north to Alexandria in the south. It was, in fact, the Byzantine world. For business purposes at least Greek was still the lingua franca of that world, just as Orthodoxy was the common form of Christianity. Its center was still Constantinople. The Phanariotes were not very interested in the idea of setting up a Hellenic Republic. Their dream of liberation from the Turks involved nothing less than the recreation of the Byzantine Empire. They looked to Moscow and to Bucharest for the fulfillment of that dream, not to Greece or to the West. Moscow, the Third Rome, seat of an Orthodox Patriarch and an Orthodox Tsar, was the "white hope" for the liberation of the Byzantine people. The liberation of Greece could wait until the double-headed eagle flew again in Constantinople.[24]

Catherine the Great of Russia was rather taken with this idea. Her friend Voltaire encouraged her to imagine a new Russian Empire with Constantinople, not Moscow, as its capital. This is surely not what the Greeks had in mind. But Catherine was interested in the Greek cause as well; and she toyed with the idea of a Greek Empire too—or rather an Orthodox Empire, which would comprise the Slav as well as the Greek Christian populations of European Turkey. It would be centered on Constantinople, and its first emperor would be her own grandson Constantine. There were some who could already hear the bellowing of the ox and the stirring of the sleeping giant at the Golden Gate of the City. Once again Orthodoxy, not Hellenism, was to be the test of nationality. But it was all fantasy. The Greeks were quickly and sadly disillusioned by Catherine's only direct intervention in their affairs. During the course of the Russo-Turkish War that she instigated in 1768, a small Russian force landed at Navarino to help rouse the Greeks of the Peloponnese to rebellion. It was massacred in 1770, and the Turkish reprisals were terrible. More and more the Greeks looked to the West for their salvation.[25]

The Orthodox Church would probably have approved of the reestablishment of an Orthodox empire centered at Constantinople, if it had ever come about. But when the real Greek War of Independence finally began, the Church at once registered its disapproval. In March 1821 an encyclical was posted in all the Greek churches in Constantinople. It was signed by the Patriarch Gregory, the Patriarch of Jerusalem, and twenty-one other Orthodox bishops. It excommunicated all those responsible for taking up arms in revolution against the protector of Christians and the lawful sovereign of the Ottoman Empire, the Sultan. "For there is no power but of God; the powers that be are ordained of God, and he who objects to this Empire...rebels against God's order."[26] This was pure Byzantine political thought, unchanged and unadulterated. It did not save the Patriarch Gregory. The Turks laid the responsibility for the rebellion at his door, as head of the Christian *millet*; and they hanged him at the gate of his palace in the Phanar. Fourteen of his bishops suffered the same fate.[27]

The Greek rebellion, or War of Liberation, did in the end result in the establishment of a monarchy in Greece, western style. It was not the Byzantine Empire of the Romans revived; it was the Kingdom of the Hellenes. The protection of the Orthodox faith was enshrined in the first article of its Constitution. Nonetheless, it was a Hellenic and not a Byzantine kingdom. This was what the western powers had wanted and expected; and for a time, largely due to western influence, Hellenism duly prevailed in Greece. King Otto was a Bavarian, no more Orthodox by birth than Catherine the Great had been. His German architects went to work to make a mini-Munich out of Athens. Only at the last moment were they dissuaded from turning the Parthenon into a royal palace. His Greek subjects enthusiastically recreated all the administrative apparatus of ancient Athens—an Areopagos, a Boule, an Academy, nomarchs, demarchs, and the rest. Slav or Turkish place names were altered to their supposed ancient forms to make the new Hellenes feel more at home. The advice of Koraes was followed with regard to the Greek language. It was purged of its impurities so drastically that almost no one could write it any more, let alone speak it. Even the Church of Greece became a national, Hellenic institution, autocephalous and independent of the jurisdiction of the Patriarch of Constantinople. And then came Constantine Paparregopoulos with his monumental *History of the Greek Nation*, first published in five volumes between the years 1860 and 1872. His purpose was to point the moral that, after all, Hellenism and Byzantinism, the ancient and the medieval traditions of the Greek people, were one and the same in spirit.

There was a historical continuum between Homer and King Otto of Bavaria. The Byzantines, or rather the Byzantine Greeks, had been Hellenes at heart, though sometimes regrettably led astray by oriental influences. The marriage of Hellenism and Christianity had, at length, been celebrated in the Christian Kingdom of the Hellenes.

Generations of modern Greeks have been brought up on the great *History* of Paparregopoulos. It has inspired them with a sense of the unity and continuity of their race; and it is perhaps presumptuous for foreigners to question the validity of a national myth so ably and often poetically expressed. But it is a fact that the roots of the new Hellas of the nineteenth century were still firmly planted in the Byzantine Orthodox tradition. Hellenism was something strange and foreign. People who lived in Vodena, Karavassara, or Velestino were puzzled when they were told to rename their towns with the ancient names of Edessa, Amphilochia, and Pherai. The heroes of Homer, of Athens, of Sparta, and of Thebes were no doubt splendid warriors. But the Christian soldier-saints of Byzantium painted on the walls of the local church were nearer, more familiar, and more comforting. One only had to enter an Orthodox church to be wafted back into the half-remembered glory of the Byzantine Empire. The paintings and icons recalled that strange but familiar blend of Byzantine imperial and celestial mystery, from the all-seeing eyes of the Christ Pantokrator in the dome, to the Virgin in the apse, to the figures of Constantine the Great, the first Christian Emperor, with his mother Saint Helena, robed and crowned and haloed like a holy emperor and empress. Every church, however humble, enclosed a piece of heaven. Every church was a microcosm of the Great Church of Hagia Sophia in Constantinople.

It is easy to see how the idea grew that the establishment of the kingdom or nation of the Hellenes was only a beginning. When, in February 1821, Alexander Hypsilantis called on the Greeks to rise up and shed the blood of the tyrant Turks, he reminded them of the brave deeds of such as Epaminondas, Miltiades, Themistocles, and Leonidas.[28] Hypsilantis made his famous proclamation not in Thebes or in Athens, but in Romania. He was a Phanariote Greek who had been prince across the Danube. He had also served in the cavalry of the Russian Tsar. He liked to roll out the names of ancient Greek warriors and heroes. Most of his audience had little idea of what he was talking about, but they loved the rhetoric of it all. Hypsilantis sincerely wanted to turn the Turks out of Greece. But that was only the first step. For him, as for so many others at the time, the ultimate goal was Constantinople. His proclamation begins with the stirring words: "Fight for Faith and Fatherland!" But where, for Greek-speakers of the Orthodox faith, was the fatherland? This question has bedevilled the entire history of the post-Byzantine world.

Koraes would probably have agreed that the true line of continuity between Homer and King Otto, or between Mycenaeans, Hellenes, Byzantines, and modern Greeks, is that of the Greek language. This is the current that has never been cut off, in spite of numerous historical interruptions. Greek has persisted longer than any other language except for Chinese. The problem in post-Byzantine, or even post-classical, history has been where to locate the center of its supply. Was it Athens or Constantinople or Bucharest or Jassy or Odessa or Alexandria or Smyrna or Ayvalik? The Greek-speaking and Byzantine-thinking world was so scattered. The Ottoman Empire, after all, covered almost exactly the same geographical area as the Byzantine Empire; and its Greek-speaking Christian inhabitants had been designated from the start as the "Greek Nation," the *millet-i Rum*, of Orthodox Christians. But what would be the limits of that nation, and what would be its center, once it became independent?

For many years after the war that secured the independence of Greece, the fatherland, the *patris* of the Greek-speaking people was held to be Constantinople. Their identity as Hellenes was not enough. Hellenism was only one of their roots. They were also Romaioi, or Byzantines. That part of their identity required the possession of Constantinople as well as Athens. Their Byzantine tradition was indeed closer and more alive than that of ancient Greece. The continuity of the Greek cultural heritage, as of the living Orthodox heritage, must therefore, be proved and achieved through the realization of a Great Idea—the *Megale Idea*—the recreation of the Byzantine Empire as a Hellenic institution. The Idea was clearly expressed by Ioannes Kolettis when addressing the Constituent Assembly in Athens in 1844:

> The Kingdom of Greece is not Greece. [Greece] constitutes only one part, the smallest and poorest part. A Greek is not only a man who lives within this kingdom. He is also one who lives in Ioannina, in Thessalonike, in Serres, in Adrianople, in Smyrna, in Trebizond, in Crete, in Samos, and in any land associated with Greek history or the Greek race.... There are two main centers of Hellenism: Athens, the capital of the Greek kingdom, [and] "the City" [Constantinople], the dream and hope of all Greeks.[29]

The Great Idea, the dream of fulfilling that hope by taking over Byzantium, fuddled the wits of Greek statesmen and politicians for about a hundred years after 1821. The bubble was finally pricked by the disaster of the Greek military adventure in Asia Minor in 1922. Greece today has accepted the smaller and less dangerous idea of being a western European nation in a community of like-minded nations. In making this adjustment it has in many ways outgrown both of its burdensome traditions, the Hellenic and the Byzantine, the ancient and the medieval. The Hellenes of antiquity never succeeded in living together in harmony as one people until unity was imposed upon them first by the Macedonians and then by the Romans. The Byzantines of the Middle Ages always thought in terms of a universal empire in which there was no place for separatism. They would have found the modern concept of nationhood undesirable and unintelligible. Ever since Lord Byron, and indeed long before, the western world has had impossibly high expectations that the Greeks would one day live up to the promise of their classical heritage. Ever since Edward Gibbon, the western world has misunderstood or despised the Byzantine heritage of the Greeks as a deadening influence. Koraes taught the Greeks themselves to feel the same. But surely both he and Gibbon were wrong. The legacy of Byzantium is no less important than that of ancient Hellas in defining the modern Greeks as Europeans. For it links them to a culture and a religion that they imparted to and shared with most of the non-Hellenic people of Eastern Europe in the Middle Ages.

NOTES

1. Georgios Sphrantzes, *Memorii 1401–1477*, ed. V. Grecu (Bucharest, 1966), pp. 446–56; Kritoboulos, ed. V. Grecu, *Critobul din Imbros* (Bucharest, 1963), pp. 173–74; S. Runciman, *The Great Church in Captivity. A Study of the Patriarchate of Constantinople from the Eve of the Turkish Conquest to the Greek War of Independence* (Cambridge, 1968), pp. 168–70.

2. C. N. Sathas, *Documents inédits relatifs à l'histoire de la Grèce au moyen âge*, 4 (Paris, 1833), p. vii.

3. Gennadios (George Scholarios), *Against the Jews*, in *Oeuvres complètes de Gennade Scholarios*, ed. L. Petit, X. A. Siderides and M. Jugie (Paris, 1928–36), 3, p. 252.

4. Kritoboulos, ed. Grecu, p. 25 lines 4–6.

5. N. G. Politis, *Meletai peri tou viou kai tes glosses tou Hellenikou laou. Paradoseis* (Athens, 1904), 1, p. 23 no. 35; 2, p. 678.

6. C. A. Mango, "The Legend of Leo the Wise," *Zbornik Radova Vizantološkog Instituta*, 6 (Belgrade, 1960), pp. 59-93. On Agathangelos: B. Knös, *L'Histoire de la Littérature Néo-Grecque*, 1: *La période jusqu'en 1821* (Uppsala, 1962), pp. 461-62.

7. Gregory Palamas, *Capita*, in Migne, 150, 1137. D. M. Nicol, "The Byzantine Church and Hellenic Learning in the Fourteenth Century," *Studies in Church History*, 5, ed. G. J. Cuming (Leiden, 1969), pp. 23-57, especially 50-51 (reprinted in D. M. Nicol, *Byzantium: Its Ecclesiastical History and Relations with the Western World. Collected Studies* [London, Variorum 1972], no. 12).

8. Runciman, *Great Church in Captivity*, pp. 271-74; G. A. Hadjiantoniou, *Protestant Patriarch. The Life of Cyril Lucaris* (Richmond, Va., 1961), pp. 78-90.

9. Catherine Koumarianou, "The Contribution of the Intelligentsia towards the Greek Independence Movement, 1798-1821," in R. Clogg, ed., *The Struggle for Greek Independence. Essays to Mark the 150th Anniversary of the Greek War of Independence* (London, 1973), pp. 70-71.

10. K. Spetsieris, "Eikones Hellenon Philosophon eis ekklesias," *Epistemonike Epeteris tes Philosophikes Scholes tou Panepistemiou Athenon*, 14 (1963-64), 386-458.

11. T. Koloktronis, *Apomnemoneumata*, ed. T. Vournas (Athens, n.d.) p. 70.

12. A. Politis, "He prosgraphomene ston Riga prote ekdose tou Agathangelou. To mono gnosto antitypo," *O Eranistis*, 7 (1969), pp. 173-92.

13. The Revolutionary Proclamation and the New Political Constitution 17 of Rigas Velestinlis are translated in R. Clogg, ed., *The Movement for Greek Independence 1770-1821. A Collection of Documents* (London, 1976), pp. 149-63. See D. A. Zakythinos, *The Making of Modern Greece: From Byzantium to Independence* (Oxford, 1976), pp. 157-67.

14. C. Th. Dimaras, *A History of Modern Greek Literature*, translated by Mary P. Gianos (New York, 1972; London, 1974), pp. 189-211; G. P. Henderson, *The Revival of Greek Thought 1620-1830* (Albany, N.Y., 1970), pp. 142-69; Zakythinos, *Modern Greece*, pp. 174-77.

15. A. Toynbee, *The Greeks and Their Heritages* (Oxford, 1981), pp. 233-34.

16. Cited by K. Krumbacher, *Geschichte der byzantinischen Literatur* (Munich, 1897), Preface, p.v.

17. Knös, *L'Histoire*, pp. 504-13; Zakythinos, *Modern Greece*, pp. 107-8, 154; Henderson, *The Revival*, pp. 69-74.

18. Zakythinos, *Modern Greece*, pp. 168-70; Dimaras, *A History*, pp. 136-40.

19. Zakythinos, *Modern Greece*, pp. 170-71.

20. The *Paternal Exhortation* of 1798 is translated in Clogg, *The Struggle*, pp. 56–64; Runciman, *Great Church in Captivity*, pp. 394–95.

21. P. Sherrad, *The Greek East and the Latin West. A Study in the Christian Tradition* (Oxford, 1959), pp. 179–86; Toynbee, *The Greeks*, pp. 251–64.

22. A. F. Didot, *Notes d'un Voyage fait dans le Levant en 1816 et 1817* (Paris, 1826), pp. 385–87; translated in Clogg, *The Struggle*, pp. 80–81.

23. Translated in Clogg, *The Struggle*, pp. 86–88.

24. Runciman, *Great Church in Captivity*, pp. 360–84; C. Mango, "The Phanariots and the Byzantine Tradition," in Clogg, *The Struggle*, pp. 41–66.

25. C. M. Woodhouse, *Modern Greece: A Short History* (London, 1968), pp. 118–21.

26. Anathematization of the *Philike Etairia* by the Patriarch Gregory V, translated in Clogg, *The Struggle*, pp. 203–6.

27. *Ibid.*, pp. 206–8.

28. *Ibid.*, pp. 201–3.

29. Kolettis, cited by R. Clogg, "The Greek *Millet* in the Ottoman Empire," in B. Braude and B. Lewis , eds., *Christians and Jews in the Ottoman Empire. The Functioning of a Plural Society*, 1 (New York, 1982), p. 193.

PART THREE

Greece in Transition

THE CONTINUITY OF GREEK CULTURE

Bernard M. W. Knox

MY TITLE IS obviously over ambitious. The continuity of Greek culture is a vast and complex field of study, demanding of its practitioners expertise in ancient, Byzantine, and Modern Greek language, literature, and history; of Slavic and Turkish language and history; of the ritual and theology of the Orthodox Church, and a score of related disciplines, more in fact than one scholar can master in a lifetime. It is also an area of continuing interest and controversy. As recently as 1981, for example, the Hellenic Cultural Centre in London organized a panel discussion on the theme "3000 Years of Greek Identity." The three panels, chaired by the Byzantine scholar, Robert Browning, were addressed by three Greeks brought up outside Greece, three Greeks raised in Greece, and three English scholars; one of the talks by Costa Carras "3000 Years of Greek Identity—Myth or Reality?" was published in London in 1983. And it is a field in which fresh data are constantly supplied to feed fresh discussion.

Even in one narrow field, the continuity of the language, Professor Shipp, an Australian scholar who is a noted authority on the language of Homer, published a book entitled *Modern Greek Evidence for the Ancient Greek Vocabulary* and in 1974 Nikolaos Andriotis, working in the opposite direction, published in Vienna, his *Lexicon der Archaismen in neugriechischen Dialekten*. Here indeed are to be found 3000 years, or more, of Greek identity. The language inscribed on the fire-baked clay tablets found at Pylos on the mainland and at Knossos on Crete, dating from about 1600 B.C., is recognizably a primitive form of the language in which the newspapers of Athens are written today. Of course, in this immense stretch of time, the language has undergone many changes, but no other European language even comes close to claiming such a longevity; the only real parallel, in fact, is Chinese.

The profusion of studies published on this and all the other aspects of the long Greek tradition is such that any deluded speaker who thinks he can build a bridge between ancient and modern Greece in a forty-five minute lecture will end up constructing a shaky structure at best and may find himself lamenting, like the bridge builder in the famous medieval Greek ballad:

αλίμονο στους κόπους μας, κρίμα στη δούλεψή μας
ὁλομερὶς να χτίζουμε, τὸ βράδυ να γκρεμειέ ται

Alas for our trouble, alas for our work,
To build it all day long, and have it collapse at night.

I shall aim lower. What I would like to do is to speak about my own encounter with modern Greece, its language and culture, the encounter of a classical literary scholar, brought up on Homer and Sophocles, with the Greece of Karamanlis and Papandreou—the elder Papandreou, I may add—I first went to Greece in 1958. I should begin by explaining that I grew up in England, where I learned ancient Greek at school in London and then went on to St. John's College in Cambridge to read Classics in the early thirties of this century.

The training I received was rigidly linguistic in emphasis (and, in that, was quite typical). The method seemed to have been designed with an eye to producing scholars who could write near-perfect Platonic verse and correct (but dull) Sophoclean iambic verse. I went through three years of Cambridge with the general impression that all the Greek worth reading came to a full stop with Theocritos (though there was, of course, the New Testament, but *that* was something for people studying Divinity) and, furthermore, that Greek history came to a stop with the death of Alexander the Great in 323 B.C. (after that, it was Hellenistic history). Towards the end of my career at Cambridge, I discovered that a friend of mine, who had chosen archaeology as his special field and was on his way to the British School in Athens, was studying, from a German handbook (there was not one in English), modern Greek. After talking to him and looking at the book, I asked my tutor whether perhaps an acquaintance with modern Greek might be useful. "Not only will it not be useful," he said, "the only people who use it are archaeologists who have to go there.

Not only will it not be useful, it will corrupt your prose style and you will end up writing Greek that sounds like Polybios."

This Olympian disdain for people who actually went to modern Greece and did not *have* to go there was no new thing; in the spring of 1877, Oscar Wilde, then an undergraduate reading Greats at Magdalen College, Oxford, went on a trip to Greece with Professor Mahaffy of his former college, Trinity College, Dublin; they saw the excavations at Olympia, the temple at Bassae, Argos, Aegina, and Athens. Unfortunately for Wilde, he returned to Oxford three weeks late for the beginning of the term. "Voyages to Greece," says his biographer, Richard Ellman, "were not common in the seventies of the last century. That they were necessary to a classical course in Oxford was more than Magdalen was ready to concede." Wilde was temporarily suspended for the rest of the academic year and deprived of his scholarship money. "I was sent down from Oxford," he said later, "for being the first undergraduate to visit Olympia."

This attitude, however, was not confined to the English classical establishment. Some time in the early sixties of this century, I asked a French archaeologist who had spent most of his life in Greece at the École Française whether he had read the modern Greek poets. (I had just discovered, with immense excitement, the poetry of Kavafis and Seferis.) "No," he said, "I have to know enough modern Greek to talk to the work-men on the dig, but I try to keep my acquaintance with it to a minimum— it might spoil my appreciation of the subtleties of Plato's style."

I am sorry to say that this attitude towards modern Greek and modern Greece, typical of so many scholars, especially those concerned with literature, was just as prevalent in the United States when I first began to do graduate work and then to teach at Yale after the Second World War. My colleagues spent their summers and their sabbatical years in London, Paris, Vienna, Rome—cities where there were manuscripts of ancient Greek authors to collate, where the great libraries offered immense bibliographical resources, the great cities their comforts and cultural amenities, and the universities their classical scholars for consultation and discussion. I, too, when my first fellowship allowed me to travel, in 1953, went to Rome and Florence, partly because, as a result of military service in Italy in the Second World War, I spoke Italian, but also because in Florence, the Biblioteca Laurenziana held the great manuscript of Sophocles, on whom I was working at the time. Greece was a place to

visit, perhaps, but not to stay in (like New York); those scholars who did
go contented themselves with a visit to the most important classical sites.
They returned to their universities not so much disillusioned (for they
had expected very little); rather they returned confirmed in their convic-
tion that between the Greece of Pericles and Sophocles, on the one hand,
and that of Venizelos and Seferis, on the other, (not that they knew very
much about either of these two), there was a gap so wide that little or
nothing of value to the classicist was to be learned from a closer knowledge of the life, literature, and language of modern Greece.

To the Greeks themselves, whose early training and later study reinforced their consciousness of the continuity of the Greek tradition, such
an attitude must appear bizarre, just as it would appear strange to English-
men if a foreign scholar of Chaucer or Shakespeare found nothing useful
for his studies in the language and customs of modern England. But this
attitude exists and persists and since I, too, shared it to some extent
before I had the good fortune to spend a whole year in Greece, I would
like to describe it and try to explain it. I have long since been free of it, but
the converted heretic is perhaps the most competent authority on the
beliefs he has rejected.

To begin with, there is the look of the place. No one can fail to be
overwhelmed by the beauty and mystery of the Altis at Olympia at moon-
light, or of Delphi at any hour (any hour, that is, when there are not ten
thousand tourists taking pictures) and no one can fail to be impressed by
the huge, yet delicate, beauty of the theater at Epidaurus; the long gallery
in the fortress at Tiryns; the splendid, somehow haunted, site of Agamem-
non's palace at Mycenae; the tomb of the Athenian and Plataean dead on
the plain where "Marathon looks on the sea." But these are secluded
ancient sites, where the scholar can easily imagine himself in the Greece
of classical or archaic times. The rest of Greece, however, is another
kettle of fish. The scholar of Greek literature who manages to find his way
behind the Larisa Station to what was Kolonos Hippios, with the marvel-
ous lines of Sophocles ringing in his ears:

εὐίππου ξένε, τᾶσδε χώρας ἵκου τὰ κράτιστα, γᾶς ἔπαυλα,
τὸν ἀργῆτα Κολωνόν, ἔνθ' ἁ λίγεια μινύρεται ... ἀηδών

Stranger, you have come to the land of fine horses, to earth's fairest
home, white Kolonos, where the nightingale, a permanent guest, trills
her clear notes in green glades, amid the wine-dark ivy in the gods'

sacred wood, heavy with fruit and berries, shaded from the sun, shielded from wind and weather.

is in for a terrible shock; what he will find at the end of the bus ride has little to do with horses and still less to do with nightingales. And suppose he tries to follow Socrates and Phaedros out to the shady spot where they talked by the river Ilissos.

> "This plane tree is spreading and tall," says Plato's Socrates, "and there is a lovely shade from the high branches of the agnus; now that it is in full flower, it will make the place fragrant. And what a lovely stream under the plane tree! and how cool to the feet . . . and the freshness of the air and the shrill summery music of the cicadas. And as a crowning delight, this grass, thick on the gentle slope, just right to rest your head on it most comfortably."

Our scholar will be a very clever man if he can find the Ilissos at all, and a very disappointed one if he does. Reluctantly, dodging traffic at every intersection, he makes his way back to the Acropolis, where, even though it is scarred and broken, there is enough left of the Parthenon and the Propylaea to remind him of the glories of Periclean Athens.

Outside Athens things are not much better. Our scholar's first view of Salamis and the straits in which the Greek fleet, watched by Xerxes from his throne, routed and sank the Persian galleys, will probably include the rusting hulks lying at anchor off Skaramangas; and all the way to the site of the Eleusian Mysteries at Eleusis he will have to look at the plume of white smoke from the huge Herakles cement factory. Where are the pine trees on the Theban mountains, the haunts of Dionysos and his maenads, of nymphs and satyrs? Where is the narrow pass that Leonidas and his three hundred Spartans held against the Persian hordes? (It would take an army corps to hold it now.) Where are the bees of Hymettos? The birds of Aristophanes? The seven gates of Thebes? Only in the books the scholar knows so well and to which he returns with relief. The first impressions of modern Greece, and particularly Athens, are enough to convince most scholars that they will understand the culture and litera- ture of the fifth century B.C. much better working in a study in Oxford or New Haven than they ever will sitting in a *kafeneion* near Plateiatis Omonoias or riding the bus to Levadia.

Then there are the people, the Greeks themselves. To the visiting scholar, they are the kindest and most solicitous of hosts (particularly in the country where their hospitality can be overwhelming), hard-working, honest, and admirable people but, thinks the scholar, they do not *look* like the ancient Greeks. He has come to Greece for the first time with the idealized faces of the young men on the Parthenon frieze stamped on his memory, his mind full of Homeric tags like *Xanthos, Menelaos*, a phrase that, particularly if he is of Anglo-Saxon or Germanic stock, he has been taught to translate "blond Menelaos." In Athens, he finds himself in a world of men and women who seem to be a startling contrast to the ideal faces which have haunted the imagination since he first saw them in the British Museum, of people who bear no resemblance to the gods and goddesses whose exquisitely proportioned features, set in the eternity of marble gilded by time, first drew him to his lifelong study of Greek.

And finally there is the language. He knows that it has changed somewhat in 2,500 years but still feels a certain confidence. After all, he has often successfully plowed his way through scholarly articles in modern Greek and occasionally read with some understanding a Greek newspaper bought in New York or London. Armed with his many years of study of ancient Greek and perhaps a few days on the boat devoted to a modern Greek phrase book, he expects to be able to manage fairly well when he gets there; after all, he has been studying Greek all his life. But the first contact with spoken Greek, especially if the speaker is a Piraeus taxi driver, can be a shattering experience. The visiting professor is reduced, like all his ignorant fellow passengers, to conducting his negotiations for a ride to Athens in what passes among Piraeus taxi drivers for English. Later, after buying a grammar and making a serious stab at the language, he begins to make some progress, but he realizes with growing despair that the reason he could read the scholarly articles and newspapers is that they are written in a Greek which tries to preserve as much of the ancient language as possible, whereas the waiters and bus drivers and policemen with whom he has to deal on his travels seem to be talking a different language. Modern Greek seems to have so little connection with the language of Demosthenes (Good Lord, it doesn't even have an *infinitive*) that he sees no point in trying to learn it.

On my first visit to Greece, once comfortably ensconced in a hotel in Iannina (we had arrived on a ferry from Brindisi to Igoumenitza), I displayed my knowledge of Greek by translating the headlines of the newspaper to my wife. But the balloon was soon punctured when she said: "Since you seem to know the language so well, why don't you call up and get us two more pillows and one more towel?" The language of Sophocles and Aristophanes was no help: my best effort—φέρετέ μου ἕνα λινὸν καὶ δύο προσκεφ άλαια—was answered by a series of excited questions which, unfortunately, I could not understand and I was reduced to the expedient of going down to the desk and using sign language.

These first impressions are, of course, my own; but I am sure, from comparing notes with colleagues, that they are fairly representative. Unfortunately, not many scholars of ancient Greek literature have the opportunity that was offered to me—to stay on for a whole year and find that these first impressions, like most first impressions, were unreliable.

First, the land itself. It is true that the country has changed enormously since the fifth century but we forget that many of the things we complain of were already a cause for concern in ancient times such as deforestation. In Plato's dialogue, *Critias*, the Athenian aristocrat after whom the dialogue is named, draws a nostalgic contrast between present and past. "What now remains compared with what existed then," he says, "is like the skeleton of a sick man, all the fat and soft earth wasted away and only the bare framework of the land left . . . The country was once unspoiled: its mountains were arable highlands and what is now stony fields was once good soil. And the earth was enriched by the annual rains that were not lost as now by flowing from the bare land into the sea . . . but deep soil received and stored the water . . . there were forests on the mountains; there are some that now have nothing but food for bees, that had trees not so very long ago, and the rafters from those that were chopped down to roof the large buildings are still sound." And there are many features of Greek soil and climate that have never changed, the weather, for example. One has to live through a Greek summer to know why Pindar began his first Olympian ode with the bald statement, ῎Αριστον μεν ὕδωρ, "Water is best." I first read that line in England, where water is so plentiful that sometimes there does not seem to be anything else (someone once suggested that Thales, with his theory that all things are water, must have spent some time in England) and the line does not seem to make much sense. (Some schoolboy wit had, in fact, proposed a correction to the text in my book, ζύθος for ὕδωρ, to produce the meaning: "Beer is best.") It is only in Greece that one feels the true force of that magnificent opening phrase, when one has come, like the Greeks themselves, to prefer a glass of water in the heat to beer or lemonade or wine, to call, at the *kafeneion*, for more and more *neraiki*; only a Greek summer and the total dehydration two hours in the sun can produce will make you feel the full force of Pindar's words. But this is only one small example. One has to experience a Greek thunderstorm, with the lightening visible for miles and the thunder crash echoing from mountain to mountain through the clear air to feel the terror and majesty of the last scenes of *Oedipus at Colonus*, to know what is meant by the thunderbolt Zeus brandishes with his right arm. And the sea does not change. Standing on the Acropolis looking down on the Gulf at sunset, one can see what looks like wide tracks in the pattern of rough sea and smooth; they are surely Homer's "paths of the sea" (ὑγρὰ κέλευθα). And one has to walk the bare Attic hills in the spring and see the incredible carpet of richly colored wild flowers springing from barren rock to understand why Pindar called Athens "violet crowned." With time, as the seasons change, as the olives are shaken from the trees, gathered and pressed, as the soil is plowed and sown, as much later the fruit begins to ripen and fall, as the grain is winnowed on the high circular threshing floor that must be the origin of the orchestra in which the tragic chorus danced, the scholar who has had the good fortune to spend a whole year in Greece can learn to feel the rhythm of the Greek seasons, of the Greek earth, a rhythm unlike that of his own country and one that has not changed since Hesiod wrote its rulebook and its praise.

So much for the land, but what of the people? The initial disappointment most Greek scholars feel when confronted for the first time by modern Greeks en masse is due solely to the illusions they bring with them. England and Germany were the two great centers of Greek studies in the nineteenth century and both nations created a vision of the ancient Greeks that had more to do with their ideal of themselves than with reality. In this they were encouraged by the fact that ancient Greek art was known to the nineteenth century mainly in the form of sculpture; Attic vases, which came mostly from Etruscan tombs, were labeled "Etruscan" vases until late in the century. And sculpture, at any rate the unpainted marbles of the Parthenon frieze, allows the beholder to clothe its reticent surface in any colors he pleases. "If horses had gods, they would look like horses," Xenophanes blandly observed long ago; and one has only to turn to the trashiest kind of English and American novels—the surest evidence of a people's deep-seated prejudices and most widely accepted clichés—to find what image of the ancient Greeks was formed in the Western mind. In such novels, the hero is described, as often as not, as looking "like a Greek god." Investigation of the text generally reveals that he is a little over six feet tall and has blue eyes and pale golden hair. He looks, in fact, exactly like the Edwardian ideal of the Oxford undergraduate. No wonder the first sight of the crowds in Piraeus by day and Omonoia by night give the Western classicist a jolt.

There is really no reason why it should. The vases with their black-haired and black-bearded figures, and still more, the painted archaic sculpture in the Acropolis museum, give a picture of ancient Greeks who look startlingly like the modern article. There is one *kore* in that museum, with black abundant hair and dark, wide eyes, whose modern sisters can be seen any day of the week walking down Hodos Stadiou. And, in any case, the ancient literature gives no basis for this Western feeling (sublim-inal but, therefore, stronger) that ancient Greeks were tall, blond, and blue-eyed. "Xanthos Menelaos" *may* have been blond, though the word more likely means "red-" or "brown-haired," but surely the fact that he is so often called "Xanthos" suggests that the other Achaian chieftains were not. And in Sophocles' *Antigone*, when the chorus wants to say, "ever since I became an old man," they say "ever since my hair changed from *black* to white" (ἐχ ὅτου λευκὴν ἐγὼ τενδ' ελ μέλαινες ἀμφιβάλλομαι θρίχα).

It is, of course, not only in his looks that the modern Greek resembles his ancestors. The men sitting in the *kafeneion* discussing the latest rumors and playing interminable games of *tavli* are no different from the men sitting by the fountain in Corinth playing *pessoi* (it seems to have been almost exactly the same game) from whom the *paedagogos* in Euripides' *Medea* picked up the rumor that his mistress was to be banished. The ancient Greeks were famous racers, especially in chariots; anyone who is about to take his first taxi ride in central Athens would do well to prepare himself psychologically by reading the description of the chariot race in Sophocles' *Elektra*. I once thought of writing a Pindaric ode in praise of a driver who got me through rush hour traffic to the station mainly by driving on the sidewalks. To strike a more serious note, the same touchy sense of personal honor, which is at the root of Achilles' wrath, still governs relations between man and man in modern Greece; Greek society still fosters in the individual a fierce sense of his privileges, no matter how small, of his rights, no matter how confined, of his personal worth, no matter how low. And to defend it, he will stop, like Achilles, at nothing. Even its name is still the same, φιλότιμο, φιλοτιμία.

And, of course, on the larger scale of national politics, little has changed; modern Greek politics have no better analyst than Thucydides, whose somber description of Athens in the last decades of the fifth century B.C. reads like a foreshadowing of the tragic events of 1940–50. The more one lives in modern Greece, the more one is forced to see the modern in the light of the ancient and also to reread the ancient Greeks with new insights drawn for a knowledge of the modern.

And lastly, the language. It is in some ways the most rewarding aspect of modern Greece for the classical scholar. A closer study of the spoken language reveals an intimate and live relationship between the languages of fifth- and twentieth-century Athens. Not only can the modern spoken language be called on to elucidate obscure words in ancient authors, as has been brilliantly done in some passages of Aristophanes, but also the scholar who learned his Greek as a dead language has, in modern Greece, the exhilarating experience of finding it alive: he can hear in the *laiki*, the open-air market, near Kolonaki every Friday the very tone of Aristophanes' sausage seller and market women, and on the docks of Piraeus, the sharp wit and banter of the sailors who manned the great fleets which set out from what is now Passalimani.

All the scholar has to do is to forget the artificial *katharevousa* of the newspaper editorials and government bureaucracy and listen to and learn from the popular speech of Greece, which is also, of course, the base from the poets work. I ran up against the difficulties involved in the "language question" halfway through my year in Greece, which was 1960–61.

I had already been appointed Director of Harvard's Center for Hellenic Studies in Washington but had not yet taken up its responsibilities. Professor Bakalakis of the University of Thessalonike had somehow heard about the Center and also tracked me down (I was keeping away from academic circles so that I could get some work done); he invited me to come to Thessalonike to make a speech explaining what the Center was. It was a good opportunity to try out my newly learned modern Greek and also perhaps to recruit some Greek fellows for the Center (and, in fact, over the next twenty years, no less than five young scholars came from Thessalonike to spend a year at the Center). I accepted and started to work on my speech.

On the overnight train going up to Thessalonike I suddenly got cold feet. There I was, going to speak in the *dimotiki* I had learned talking to ordinary Athenians, to an academic audience on an academic subject. They might well think it, coming from a foreigner, presumptuous, even insulting. At the last stop before Thessalonike, Larisa I think it was, I bought a whole clutch of newspapers and with the help of the editorials rewrote the speech in flowing *katharevousa*.

Next morning, at 7:00 o'clock, we arrived. I had an appointment with Linos Politis at 10:00, so I walked around the town, especially along the magnificent seafront. My bag, however, was getting to be a nuisance. I happened to see the American Express office, went in and explained my situation, and asked if they could keep my bag for me, which, very courteously, they agreed to do.

Six or seven hours later, after a fascinating interview with Linos Politis, and a magnificent lunch in a restaurant on the waterfront, I was taken to my hotel for a rest before the speech and asked my host to stop by the American Express office. To my horror, here was a big sign on the door Κ Λ Ε Ι Σ Τ Ο. What is more, it was not going to open again until 6:00—too late for me. The speech was due at 5:30. So, once at the hotel, instead of a rest, I had to recompose the speech, in double quick time and this time there was no fooling around with the *katharevousa*.

The speech went off well. I had inserted two jokes to test the audience's comprehension of my imperfect accent—and they laughed at both places. Afterwards at dinner, I told Politis what had happened. For a moment, I thought he looked shocked and that I had made a mistake to tell him, but then he began to laugh. He laughed very loudly and went on laughing. And finally he said to me, "Your lucky *daimon* was at work. Leaving that second version at American Express was the best thing you could have done." And he proceeded to explain that Thessalonike was, so to speak, the home and champion of *demotiki*, was writing its grammar and syntax—"if you had tried your warmed-up *katharevousa* on the audience, they would have tried hard not to laugh." I told him that I had been suddenly terrified by the memory of a professor of law at the University of Athens who had dominated an Athenian dinner party with long discussions in a very high-flying *katharevousa*; he had been told I was a professor of ancient Greek and informed me that when he went to Munich, the German professor there told him he spoke like Plato. "Oh," said Politis, in a tone of good-humored patience. "Athens . . ."

Even this distinction between an official quasi-literary language and popular speech goes back to antiquity; we still have handbooks written in the Roman imperial period that specify lists of acceptable "Attic" words and rule out others. And we know, from the private letters that have emerged, written on papyrus, from the sands of Egypt, that Greeks there in the second century A.D. were speaking a Greek that had sometimes startling resemblances to the modern article. A boy's letter to his father, for example, in which the child asks to be taken along on his father's trip to Alexandria, begins, exactly as a modern schoolboy might begin: "Λιπόν, πάτερ μου . . ." ("Well, father . . ."). Not only is the word λοιπόν (as it was spelled in fifth-century Athens and still is) used in its modern sense of "Well, . . . ," the boy's phonetic spelling shows that the itacism that is such a pronounced feature of the modern language had already begun.

    "It is strange," says George Thomson in his brilliant book, *The Greek Language*, "that so many scholars visiting Greece to refresh themselves at the fount of Hellenism should spend all their time contemplating the material remains of antiquity without realizing that the object of their quest still flows from the lips of the people." In this aspect of modern Greece are great treasures of new insight and fresh understanding ready for the classical scholar to discover, and without the pains of excavation. All he has to do is learn and listen. And also read, for the great poets of modern Greece—and Western Europe is slowly realizing that they are among the world's greatest poets—Cavafy, Seferis, Sikelianos, Elytis, Kazantzakis, all of them are heirs to the legacy of ancient Greece that is both a blessing and a burden; all of them draw strength from the tradition even as they try to maintain their independence from it.

    What modern Greece offers the student of Classical literature and thought is just as great as, if not greater than, what it offers the archaeologist. It can renew and refresh his contact with the ancient sources in hundreds of ways. Above all, he can ground in Greek earth that Nephelokykyggia, the "ideal" Greece he has conjured up from books; it will enable him at last "to give to airy nothing a local habitation and a name."

PART FOUR

Greece: The Modern Era

GREECE IN THE SECOND WORLD WAR

Sir David Hunt

HOW WARS START is a question that has much exercised historians ever since Thucydides wrote his sophisticated analysis of the origins and causes of the Peloponnesian War. It is much in people's minds today as they contemplate apprehensively the hostilities in the former Yugoslavia. Resistance to aggression is a frequent cause, and that is how most participants in the Second World War became involved. Britain and France, indeed, and the independent countries of the British Commonwealth were unique among the major powers because they entered the conflict on their own initiative; they declared war on Germany. Italy can also claim to have taken the initiative in declaring war on Britain and France; but that was not until the last moment, when it seemed certain that Germany had already won the war. The only compunction felt in Rome arose from the fear that the declaration might have the bad luck to come too late, weakening Italy's claim to a share in the spoils. Greece's adherence to the cause of what was later called the United Nations was due to the same reasons as with most of them, large and small: they were the victims of aggression.

Nevertheless, it is not philhellenic bias alone that makes me feel that the Greeks deserve more sympathy than the Russians, though both were hijacked into the Second World War by sudden and unannounced attack. The Soviet Union was a great power and was supposed to be able to look after itself. It had for years expected and feared a German attack, and the mere fact that the two were linked by a treaty that amounted almost to an alliance should not have caused Stalin to relax his guard. Greece was a small country faced by what was then supposed to be a great power. To resist aggression appeared to offer no advantage beyond the preservation of national honor. The astonishing thing is that the Greeks instantly and unanimously decided to resist. Apart from a few eccentric individuals,[1] nobody considered the possibility of not resisting, and foreign philhellenes who knew the country well were also convinced that Greece would choose the honorable course. This determination continued unchanged, in spite of the conflicts of opinion deriving from the Ioannis Metaxas dictatorship, throughout the heroic and victorious Italo-Greek war in Albania and throughout the occupation. Popular resistance in the country was matched by the military exploits of the Greek army in Egypt and Italy, of its navy in the Mediterranean, and of the merchant marine in all seven seas.

In Greece itself it is the war in Albania that is rated as the highest individual achievement. It was successful from the first to the last; for it was German intervention that brought it to an end after the Italians had failed to achieve anything. That success was gained against all rational expectations. The enemy was so superior in numbers and equipment that only the highest level of military competence and exuberant courage, directed by skillful staff work, could account for the repeated triumphs. It was won by Greeks alone, for the assistance of the RAF and the Royal Navy, though valued, did not have a decisive effect. For the British, especially those of us who were fortunate enough to be in Greece at that time, it was a heartening stimulus. Having fought alone for a summer and an autumn that, however memorable, were distinctly claustrophobic, we found ourselves back on European soil once more and with some solidly successful allies. It is for these reasons that I have devoted most of this essay to the Albanian campaign, and also in part because what there is of value on the subject in English is usually brief and generalized. In the hope of rescuing from oblivion a campaign that is of great interest to the military historian, I have tried to go beyond the conventional eulogy of Greece's military exploits.

Since the involvement of Greece in the war was due to Italian action, it seems sensible to begin with an account of Italian aspirations in the Mediterranean and the motives that inspired the invasion of Greece. Even before the institution of fascism in 1922, one of the principal objects of Italian foreign policy had been to control as much as possible of the Mediterranean, which Mussolini was not the first to call *mare nostrum*. Since the Italian navy was always weaker than the French, the eastern Mediterranean looked more promising as a sphere of action, and here they had already come up against the Greeks. They took the side of the Turks against Greece in 1922, when the loss of the Greek annexations in Asia Minor served as a pretext for Italy to retain the Dodecanese islands, repudiating earlier promises to cede them to Greece. In the Adriatic, disappointed of annexations elsewhere, Mussolini bombarded and occupied Corfu on a flimsy and fraudulent pretext.[2] Thus when in 1939 he annexed Albania—largely out of jealousy of Hitler's central European acquisitions—Greece felt dangerously threatened. It was the first time it had shared a border with a great power. Assurances from Rome that no unfriendly action was contemplated were not taken at face value in Athens.

In the meantime, Greece had received an assurance from Britain and France on 13 April 1939,[3] similar to the one extended at the same time to Romania: on certain conditions, and if Greece resisted aggression with its own forces, the two countries would "give all the help in their power." Vague as it was, it was well received in Athens. The Greeks, with their instinctive knowledge of all sea affairs, were aware that their security depended on being on good terms with the principal naval power; besides, since the time of Byron there had been a fairly general feeling of closeness to the British, based not only on history but also on psychological similarities.

When, after the defeat of France, Italy declared war on France and Britain, the foreign minister, Ciano, profusely declared to all the remaining neutral countries of Europe that it was not his intention to drag any of them into the war. Things looked worse for Greece when the terms of the French armistice became known. Although Admiral Cunningham, commanding the British Mediterranean Fleet, had already shown his strategic skill and pugnacity by successfully engaging the Italian main battle fleet off Calabria (much assisted by the Italian airforce's bombing of their own ships), most professional opinion generally believed, on strategical grounds, that the British had lost control of the Mediterranean. This was not the view taken by Admiral Cavagnari, the Italian commander-in-chief, a cautious man, or by the Greek navy, which gave greater weight to tradition than to statistics.

Though these sensible judgments were to be vindicated before long, in midsummer 1940 the Greeks became more and more convinced of Italy's hostile intentions. They had tangible evidence to support their apprehensions. Much of it derived not from Rome but from Rhodes, from the overheated imagination of the governor of Dodecanese. Cesare-Maria de Vecchi, one of the original fascist quadrumvirate, was quarrelsome and senile but still insatiably ambitious. He bombarded Rome with long signals containing false and, indeed, fantastic reports of British warships in Greek waters.[4] To back his stories with deeds, he sent aircraft to attack Greek naval vessels in the Gulf of Corinth and in the Saronic Gulf, in sight of Athens. Finally, in spite of direct orders from Badoglio as chief-of-staff of the armed forces, he sent a submarine to the Cyclades: on 15 August it torpedoed the Greek light cruiser *Helli* in the harbor of Tinos, where it was acting as a guard ship for a religious festival. His postwar memoirs revealed that this time he had obtained authorization from Cavagnari and from Mussolini. This story is very probably true, and it illustrates the confusion and inefficiency that the "leadership principle" always produces. The outrage was a little premature, and had to be denied; but the Greeks took the warning seriously in the light of a furious Italian campaign about the murder in southern Albania of a man called Daut Hodja, described by the opposing sides as an Albanian patriot and as a sheep-stealer. The latter, at least, was correct.

Public opinion in Italy was therefore prepared for another triumph, and in Albania the military and civilian authorities were exuberantly confident; but action was still delayed. Hitler was determined to keep war out of the Balkans, not for humanitarian reasons but to avoid possible awkwardness when he invaded Russia the next spring. He had strictly forbidden an Italian attack on Yugoslavia and indicated that he was equally opposed to one on Greece.[5] Mussolini chafed at the leash. Paradoxically, it was Hitler's occupation of Romania, designed to further his plan for preserving tranquility in the Balkans, that exasperated the Duce into launching a campaign that would result in significantly delaying the German invasion of Russia. Hitler's aim was to assume control of the Romanian oil wells, which were his main source of fuel. He had no intention of sharing this control with Italy and kept his move secret until the last possible moment. Mussolini first heard of it on 8 October and was furious. On 12 October he returned to Rome from a tour of inspection in a mood that showed his resentment had increased after three days' brooding. "Hitler faces me with *faits accomplis*," he said to Ciano. "This time I shall pay him back in the same coin: he will learn from the newspapers that I have occupied Greece. That'll put the balance straight."[6]

It is rare in history to come across so plain and unequivocal a statement of intent, and even rarer to have such an obviously genuine avowal of the motives for a disastrous decision. In the light of such candor there is little purpose in treating at length the measures taken and the opinions expressed in the subsequent two weeks. Although Mussolini told Ciano at the same time as he announced his decision that he would stick to it whatever his generals thought, adding that he would resign as an Italian if anyone made difficulties about fighting the Greeks, he at least listened to the views of his senior military officers. Badoglio, the chief-of-staff, had been made marquis of Addis Ababa for triumphs in the field, though in the army his name was more closely associated with Caporetto; he was predictably glum but also equivocal. He was not allowed to dissent and waited until July 1943 for his revenge. The vainglorious and incompetent Sebastiano Visconti-Prasca, commander-in-chief in Albania, declared that he personally had prepared the operations to occupy the whole of Greece "down to the smallest details"; it was as perfect as "humanly possible." It had originally been proposed that the invasion coincide with an offensive in Egypt designed to carry the Libyan armies from Sidi Barrani to Matruh, from where the Italian airforce could threaten the Mediterranean Fleet's base in Alexandria; but Graziani, timid and unenterprising, had insisted on waiting until December. Mussolini would accept only two days' postponement in Albania and, accordingly, the attack was launched on Greece on 28 October.

That date is as notable as any in the history of Greece, and its events are proudly commemorated to the present day. The Italian foreign affairs ministry had made preparations similar to those made by the army and equally furtively. Ciano was afraid of a premature leakage not to the Greeks, from whom little resistance was expected, but to the German ally who, it was feared, might reimpose his veto. Unlike Hitler, who regarded declarations of war as relics of old-fashioned protocol, he had decided to present (with a time-limit of three hours) an ultimatum. It was vague but minatory in its terms; it was not meant to be accepted. Accordingly, the Italian minister in Athens, Grazzi, was instructed to deliver it at 3:00 AM. on the morning of the attack. After repeating accusations about the alleged offer to the British of bases in Greek territory, it demanded immediate acceptance of free passage for an unspecified number of Italian troops and the cession for an unspecified number of strategic points. Grazzi called on Metaxas at the time indicated, at his private house in Kifissia. Metaxas received him in his dressing-gown. He read the document and merely commented, "So this is war." Greek legend has it that his reply was restricted to the word "no," *ochi* in Greek, and the Greek airforce annually traces *ochi* in smoke in the sky over Athens each year on that day. Whatever he said, the prime minister made it clear that, faced with no alternative but war, Greece would resist.

In Greek folk-memory, Metaxas's reputation is rather ambiguous. Many condemn his dictatorial rule, though by historical standards, both earlier and later, it was comparatively mild. Nevertheless, he is the leading figure in one of the most memorable encounters of the twentieth century, and that is allowed to be a redeeming feature. All Greeks approved of his conduct in such a crisis, and they were proud he represented their feelings so well. The response to the mobilization order was universally enthusiastic.

Let me first describe the nature of the terrain of the ensuing campaign. The mountains in southern Albania and in Epirus on the Greek side are abrupt and tangled and have few and poor roads. When compared with the Italian Apennines, they have a strangely primitive appearance. One feature of great strategic importance is the Pindos range. For my present purposes this can be taken as starting a little north of where the borders of Albania, Yugoslavia, and Greece meet and running north-south to the latitude of the Amvrakikos Gulf. On the east the range protects the strategic Albanian town of Koritsa; and its southern part, pierced only by one high pass at Metsovo, divides Epirus from Thessaly. To threaten their principal objectives, Salonika and Athens, the Italians would need to cross the Pindos. This, in effect, meant forcing the Metsovo pass.

The weather at the end of October was likely to be unfavorable for rapid movement or for large-scale air operations. The Italians, for nonmilitary reasons, had began their aggression too late. The start was marked by several days of heavy rain, which soon turned to snow. Though better equipped for bad weather than the Greeks, they had neither a knowledge of the country nor high morale and skill in mountain warfare.

It might have been thought that given the indented nature of the Greek coastline the Italian navy, operating in its home waters in overwhelming strength and with land-based air cover, would have made a decisive contribution to the campaign. If Mussolini had been Winston Churchill he would have planned a dozen amphibious operations in the opening twenty-four hours. Admiral Cavagnari preferred playing safe. He had originally proposed a landing to secure Corfu and other Ionian islands, but when the weather deteriorated on D-Day he declared that the sea was far too rough.[7] In the event, the *Regia Marina* played no part at all in the Greco-Italian war apart from the lift it provided Allied morale with its defeats at Taranto and Matapan.

The *Regia Aeronautica* faithfully followed the theories on warfare put forth by one of its earliest commanders, Giulio Douhet. (These were also well regarded by the British and U.S. airforces.) Their first efforts were accordingly directed against Greek air and naval bases, and only thereafter turned to army support. The former effort was nugatory. The latter suffered from the difficulty of locating and effectively attacking infantry in mountains—thereby anticipating a problem still affecting the application of scientifically superior air power in an area just to the north of Albania in 1995—and failed to have any effect on the morale of steady troops who were winning at the time.

The efforts of naval and air power being thus greatly reduced, all depended—on both sides—on the army. The Italians were confident that the operation would be, as Ciano prophesied on 12 October 1940, "valuable and easy." Part of the value lay in the fact that it would be carried out without any German participation, indeed in defiance of their disapproval. The cautious Badoglio wanted to bring in the Bulgars, but when King Boris politely refused the invitation he consoled himself with the thought that a large part of the Greek army would be contained on the Bulgarian border in case Boris changed his mind. The view in Rome was that the forces available on the spot would be ample.

There were ten divisions in Albania, of which eight plus three regiments were concentrated on or near the Greek border. They had a great advantage in the initiative. The Greeks had not yet ordered mobilization; Metaxas was determined to avoid anything that could be called provocation. Consequently, on 28 October only three divisions and part of a fourth were mobilized. Two of these, accompanied by an infantry brigade, were moved closer to the Albanian border, one on each side of the Pindos range. It must be noted that a Greek division consisted of three and an Italian only of two infantry regiments. On the other hand, the Italians were more lavishly equipped, especially with artillery; an Italian division had nine batteries to the Greek six and an identical superiority in heavy mortars, which were of particular use in mountain warfare. The Italians also had the only armored force in the field, the Centauro division, equipped with light tanks that proved useful (though not decisive) in the opening phase in the coastal sector, but they were not much use in mountains. Their supply services were more than adequate. Resupply from Italy was likely to be hampered by delays in working the port of Durazzo, but the war was not expected to last long enough for this to matter.[8]

The Italian plan was to concentrate their strength on their right, in the sector west of the Pindos range. They would begin by seizing as much as possible of the relatively low-lying coastal sector and then thrust eastward to capture the Metsovo pass and gain access to the Thessalian plain. The left would hold firm in a defensive posture, ready to attempt, if all went well, a westward thrust into Macedonia aimed at Salonika. The plan was not very well conceived. Everything depended on breaking through the Pindos, a task entrusted to the 3rd Giulia Alpine division. It indicates the confidence with which the Greek resistance was expected to collapse rapidly.

The Greek strategic plan, by necessity, depended on the progress of the Italian initiative. Until mobilization could be completed, allowing them to prepare for counterattack, they had to hold firm for as long as possible on successive lines. The Greek commander-in-chief, Alexandros Papagos, insisted on one thing, however, with his mind on that eventual offensive: his extreme right should move forward to threaten the Albanian heights dominating the upper valley of the Devoli river. If he could capture Mount Morava and then descend from it on Koritsa, the pivot of enemy's line, he might dislocate the whole enemy deployment.

The opening phases of the battle went as forecast by Papagos, though disaster was only narrowly averted. West of Mount Pindos, where the weight of the Italian forces had been concentrated, the enemy made fairly good progress. The coastal plain proved suitable for Centauro's tanks, supported by ground-support fighter aircraft, and the Greeks had no antitank weapons. The initial impulse carried the Ferrara and Centauro divisions to the Kalamas river, where they seized a bridgehead but failed to exploit it. Meanwhile, at the truly vital point, the pass leading to Thessaly, the Giulia Division had come within twelve miles of Metsovo. The situation was serious. There was only one battalion available for the defense of the pass, and it was short of supplies. The weather turned to heavy snowstorms; the Italian commander was unenterprising; the civilians, including many women, formed groups of porters to carry supplies through the snow, and, when two more infantry battalions arrived, a counterattack was launched on 7 November. It was successful in first dislodging and then encircling the Giulia. Many prisoners were taken, and the remnants were forced to retire back across the border. At the same time, the pressure on the Italian defenses on Mount Morava, the spur of the Pindos that protected Koritsa from the south, was intensified.

By the end of the first week of November it was plain that a military miracle had occurred. The Italian invasion, long planned and with its great advantage of men and equipment, had been defeated. The Greeks had yielded ground on their left where it was of least value, held firm in the center, and were now advancing on their right. This would not only capture a politically and strategically important town while barring the way to an advance toward Salonika, but it would also outflank the Italian front and deprive it of an essential lateral line of communication. Speed was vital. The Greeks, now almost fully mobilized, enjoyed a temporary numerical superiority. Papagos decided that the only way to win a decisive success was to overrun the whole of Albania before Italian reinforcements could restore the balance. To this purpose he ordered the offensive to begin before full mobilized strength had been reached, and he transferred formations from Crete and from the Bulgarian border to reinforce it. The general theme was to improve his position on the right, to follow up the Italian withdrawal on the left, and to prepare for an offensive in the center that should advance on the Ioannina-Argyrokastro line aiming to capture the port of Valona. The date set for the start was 14 November; four days earlier Mussolini had assured his chiefs of staff that "fortunately the Greek army's dynamism was already exhausted."

The Greeks were in fact strikingly successful with their offensive. Morale was extremely high and correspondingly depressed on the Italian side. In the attack on the mountain defenses of Koritsa, the Greek artillery was handled with great boldness. The town fell on 23 November. Visconti-Prasca had by then been removed from his post and replaced, on 13 November, by Ubaldo Soddu, an affable, corpulent, and persuasive officer who spent his evenings in Albania composing music for films. Faced with the realities of war he was liable to take a less lighthearted view: when the Greek II Corps pushed north from Koritsa along the Yugoslav border to capture Pogradec on 30 November, he signaled to Rome that the Greeks had broken through, that no further military action was possible, and that the situation must be resolved by "a political intervention." The Duce, said Ciano, was more crushed by this than he had ever seen him. "It's absurd, grotesque, but that is how it is. I shall have to ask Hitler to arrange an armistice."[9] That was much too dramatic; however severe the Italian defeat, the mere topography of Albania ruled out any rapid collapse. The Greeks could advance only at foot's pace. Nevertheless, the mood of the Italian commander-in-chief accurately reflected the spirit of his troops. The advance on the right was now running into a cul-de-sac between the lake and mountains, but on the western front the strategic thrust planned by Papagos was now making significant gains. On 6 December Aghioi Saranda was captured; just over the Albanian border, it was useful as a supplementary supply port. It had been renamed Porto Edda in honor of Mussolini's daughter, Ciano's wife; pious Greeks augured that no good would come to the house of Mussolini for replacing the hallowed names of the Forty Martyrs of Sebasteia with a name chosen by her atheist father from Ibsen. On 8 November Argyrokastro was in Greek hands.

It was about this time that the Greeks began to feel the first tangible results of British cooperation. On 22 August Metaxas had enquired what help Greece could expect if attacked by Italy. Wavell, commander-in-chief Middle East, fully realized the strategic importance of Greece to the defense of his own position and was conscious of the moral obligation created by the Anglo-French guarantee. His forces were too weak for him to offer any army support—nor was any requested—but he appreciated that unless he could promise some air support Greek morale, especially among civilians, would be badly affected by the crushing Italian superiority. On the other hand, faced as he was by Italian forces in Libya and Ethiopia, each ten times as strong as any he could put in the field, he would find it difficult to maintain his position in Egypt—and everything depended on the security of Egypt. He could offer nothing on the ground and very little in the air. The navy would welcome a chance to engage the Italian fleet in Greek waters but, taking the situation as a whole, as he replied to Metaxas, no specific promise of assistance could be made until Egypt was secure.[10]

When the invasion came, Winston Churchill sent a telegram to Metaxas saying "We shall give you all the help in our power. We fight a common foe and we will share a common victory." As a start, on 29 October a RAF squadron of Blenheims, half fighters and half bombers, landed at Eleusis near Athens to help with the defense of the capital. On 4 November it was decided to add two Blenheim bomber squadrons and two Gladiator fighter squadrons. It was not much, though it left Egypt

seriously weak, reducing fighter strength there by a third until mid-
December and bomber strength by a half for many weeks. On 16 November the necessary support echelons arrived by sea at Piraeus (the codename, as I noticed to my surprise on preparing to embark, was Barbarity),
and an RAF headquarters was established in Athens under air commo-
dore D'Albiac. The appearance of the fighters over the Albanian front had
an encouraging effect; the bombers, following the same doctrine as the
Italian one, were used mainly to attack base areas at Valona and Durazzo.

The Italians, now thoroughly apprehensive, were reinforcing Albania as fast as they could. (Before the end of the campaign they would
increase their strength there from ten to 28 divisions.) This had disadvantages, since many of the new men were untrained. A division with a
good reputation, the Lupi di Toscana, arrived without transport or artillery and found itself, after a twenty-four hour approach march in the
snow under Greek attack near Klissoura, without orders and without
maps. Inside a week it was reduced to less than two hundred all ranks.
The unfortunate Wolves of Tuscany had been thrown ineffectively right
into the path of the main Greek thrust. Klissoura was a position immensely
strong by nature, but on 10 January 1941 it fell to an impetuous assault of
the 5th Division, brought recently from Crete from where it was mainly
recruited. It was one of the most remarkable actions of the campaign, all
the more because it was fought in a continuous snowstorm. The old
Turkish castle of Klissoura dominates the gorge of the Voioussa river;
some ten miles down the river is an even more famous castle, Tepeleni,
to which the assault now turned. It was never taken. The midwinter
weather, the difficulties of supply and transport, and the increasing
numbers of the enemy brought the advance to a halt. The Italians had
saved Valona by a narrow margin; two and a half years later they surrendered it, without fuss, to the Germans.

If the gorge of the Voioussa between Klissoura and Tepeleni marked
the limit of the Greek advance, Papagos and his soldiers were about to
demonstrate that they were equally masters of the defensive. The Italians
were desperate for some success, both to restore the morale and reputation of their army and, even more, because the German build-up in
Bulgaria was reaching the point at which they plainly must shortly attack
Greece in force. It was highly desirable politically to gain some credit
before the last chance was gone. Accordingly, twelve divisions were
assembled between the Voioussa and Osum rivers (Aōos and Apsos in

Greek) Mussolini went over to watch the triumphant progress of the offensive, codenamed *Primavera*, which began on 9 March. The Greeks on that front had only six divisions. In spite of German assistance with air supply, and despite a large increase in their artillery support, the Italians were unable to advance. The fighting was severe and often at close quarters. The RAF also went over to army support to meet this offensive. Greek casualties amounted to 1,200 dead and 4,000 wounded, Italian to 12,000 dead and wounded.[11] The offensive was abandoned on 25 March. Thereafter the Italians gave up the idea of fighting the Greeks any longer, contenting themselves with watching while the Germans took their enemies in the rear.

I am conscious that in describing in conventional strategic terms the campaign in Albania I am falling short of a true picture of its rigors. I am particularly reminded of this by an exhibition I helped to organize in London for the fiftieth anniversary of V-Day. It was a collection of over a hundred drawings and paintings by a leading artist, Alexandros Alexandrakis, who served in the Greek artillery. The mountain scenery, the horse-drawn or mule-borne artillery, the snow and the swift-flowing rivers depicted are more eloquent of the hardships than any prose. I am bearing in mind that this was also the last time large formations were engaged. The Greeks in exile could not muster more than a brigade, and their heroism deserves to be recorded.

In the Albanian campaign the Italians had been decisively defeated. In prisoners alone they lost about 23,000 men. They were rescued from their ordeal only by the fact that the German forces invading southern Yugoslavia went on to overrun the whole rear areas of the Greeks opposing them. I shall deal only shortly with the German intervention because, apart from operations northwest of Salonika, the Greeks were not involved on any large scale. It was the British, with occasional help from isolated Greek units, who conducted the retreat through mainland Greece and fought in Crete.

When Metaxas rejected the Italian ultimatum he knew that he might find himself at war with Germany as a result. Indeed, when he was asked two months later by the British ambassador whether, assuming he beat the Italians and was not attacked by the Germans, he would declare war on Germany, he replied that "he would stand by England as England had stood by Greece." On 15 January he assured Wavell, on an urgent visit to Athens, that he would never agree to a separate peace. On 29 January he died unexpectedly, as much a casualty of the war as any of the heights of Pindos.

His successor was Alexandros Koryzis, an honest but apprehensive banker. On 23 February an agreement was reached that British troops should be sent from Egypt to assist the Greeks. Churchill favored this, as he did all forward policies, but the decisive voice was Wavell's. Although it meant abandoning his conquests in Libya, for if anything like an effective force were to be sent to Greece their garrison would have to be most dangerously weakened, he took the view that wars are not won by refusing to fight. Not to come to the help of the Greeks would bring more disgrace and damage than any defeat. Koryzis had declared that they would fight the Germans in any case, even though all the British could offer were three and a half divisions; Wavell and Eden, supported by Churchill, agreed. Wavell's final appreciation quoted James Wolfe's dictum that war is "an option of difficulties." The mood among the officers and men who sailed to Greece might be likened to that in which senior French officers advanced to Waterloo, "without fear and without hope."

There was what was politely called a misunderstanding of plans. Eden and Wavell thought that Papagos had agreed to withdraw all troops from Thrace and eastern Macedonia, abandoning Salonika, and to make a stand on the line of the Aliakmon river. This position would be reinforced by troops withdrawn from Albania. His own interpretation was that such moves might not turn out to be necessary if Yugoslavia joined the Allies, as seemed possible at the time. Most postwar historians have concluded that Papagos would never have contemplated a voluntary abandonment of his conquests in Albania, and that even if he had given this order it would have proved impossible to execute it. That means that the strong Aliakmon line could be turned by the Germans from Yugoslav Macedonia. The debate has probably been more hypothetical than real. So overwhelming was the German force that invaded Greece on 6 April that the Allies could not have stopped it.

On the retreat southward, the British forces were supported by only a few Greek units from the reserves, because the victorious army in southern Albania was cut off, as were the troops along the Bulgarian front, because the Germans were able, after routing the Yugoslavs, to slip round their exposed western flank and drive to the sea at Salonika. The strong defenses of the Metaxas line had resisted all frontal attacks, although the Germans applied their usual tactical skill, backed up with flamethrowers, dive bombers, and even parachutists. After the inevitable surrender, the German army group-commander, Field-Marshal List, singled out the defenders of Fort Rupel for special commendation. "All in vain," my Cretan friend Colonel Hadjidakis said to me; I reminded him that Metaxas had said, on 15 January, "We are fighting not for victory but for honor."

As my theme is Greece, I shall not describe the way the British forces made good their retreat and were successfully taken off by the Royal Navy. Of course, this success owed much to Greek support, which was unflinching. It was also greatly assisted by the sudden success of British cryptographers in breaking the German ciphers encrypted on the *Enigma* machine. The information derived from top-level German communications, later given the codename *Ultra*, was so copious and prompt that General Wilson, the British commander, was praised far beyond his merits for his skillful conduct of the operation. For the invasion of Crete the information was equally perfect. Perhaps General Freyberg, the fabulously brave but intellectually limited commander of the Cretan garrison, did not make the best of it. I find the story of Crete so painful and depressing that I can hardly bear to reread the admirable account by our battalion medical officer.[12] We came very close to complete success. German casualties were so heavy as to shock even Hitler, and parachutists were never again employed on a large scale. But I cannot refrain from praising the courage of the Cretans. All the men of military age had gone off to Albania, and only the old and the very young were left. But they formed makeshift units, armed with pikes and ancient muskets when modern rifles were insufficient, and fought alongside us. It was one of these makeshift battalions that drove the parachutists from Rethymno airfield, at dreadful cost, with a bayonet charge. The Cretans were as courteous and helpful as they were brave. I remember when I was making my way to the south coast to take a ship away from the island, they remained supportive, sympathetic, and never reproachful. Their proud history of resistance to German occupation while avoiding dissent among themselves was an example to Greece.

With the fall of Crete, operations by Greek forces against the Axis came to an end. They were resumed later, in Egypt and in Italy, but not on the scale of the Albanian campaign. Nevertheless, they also made a vital contribution to the main structure of the war whose principal theater was always the eastern front, where Germany and Russia grappled over a wider area, and with immensely greater forces, than anywhere else.

The invasion of Russia, codenamed *Barbarossa*, had been planned since July 1940. In November the first formal directive was issued, specifying 15 May 1941 as the date by which everything was to be ready. Meanwhile, the Italians had attacked Greece. Hitler called it "a regrettable blunder." It worried him unduly because he believed the worthless German intelligence service, which maintained that the British had occupied the island of Lemnos in the northern Aegean. Lemnos, if the British had in fact occupied it, and if it had had an airfield, would have been a good base for air attacks on the Romanian oil fields. This made Hitler alter his decision. He organized a second operation, separate from and preparatory to *Barbarossa*, called *Marita*. Its object was to overrun Greece (possibly including Crete, though some have held that that was an afterthought), rescue the Italians, and overawe the Yugoslavs. That meant a subtraction from the forces massing for the main assault; but worse was to come. The Simovic coup of 17 March, which overthrew the pro-Axis government in Belgrade and signed a treaty of friendship with the Soviet government, threw Hitler into a fury. He recklessly increased the scope of the flank-guard operation, ordering back divisions that were already moving to their battlestations in Poland and diverting fresh divisions to the new front. A direct consequence, acknowledged in the Army Supreme Command orders, was that D-Day for *Barbarossa* was postponed until 22 June.[13]

It is a fact of history that the German armies stood at the gates of Moscow on 5 December 1941. They were halted by Soviet counterattacks and the onset, unusually late as it happened, of severe winter weather. If they had been able to start the campaign six weeks earlier, as they could have but for Balkan distractions, they would have had time to capture the city and perhaps change the history of the world. I acknowledge that it is unscientific to build a hypothesis on a hypothesis, but I remember that Winston Churchill used to quote the Greek effort as an illustration of Aesop's fable of the mouse and the lion, of which there is a large painting, most insecurely attributed to Rubens, in the Great Hall at Chequers. I like to think that the struggles of Greek soldiers in the Albanian mountains were in part responsible for frustrating the plans of the Nazi tyrant at the moment of his greatest strength.

After the loss of Crete, the whole of Greece was occupied by Germans, Italians, and Bulgarians. The Italians dropped out after September 1943, by which time they had carried out 8,000 executions, compared with 35,000 by the Germans, and 25,000 by the Bulgarians, both of whom stayed longer. Those imprisoned totaled 175,000 and hostages taken 88,000. Economic plunder of what has always been a rather poor country produced starvation, the main cause of a reduction in population from eight to seven million people.

Even without being provoked by the horrors of the occupation, the Greeks would always have organized resistance, true to their liberty-loving traditions. Patriotic movements sprang up in every region. By 1943 two were dominant, the National Liberation Front, whose acronym in Greek was EAM, and EDES, the National Republican Greek League. The latter consisted of liberals and anti-monarchical ex-officers and soldiers, and was mainly active in Epirus. EAM, the larger of the two, was controlled by KKE, a rigidly Stalinist party, as Professor Angelopoulos found to his annoyance. Its aim was not to fight the occupiers but to make sure that Greece became a Communist state after they had gone; in preparation for their departure, EAM devoted its time and energy to destroying all other resistance organizations, especially EDES. The only time the two collaborated was in November 1942, when they provided protective detachments for a party of British parachutists commanded by Brigadier Myers of the Royal Engineers, which destroyed a railway bridge over the Gorgopotamos river between Salonika and Athens.[14] Among the population in general there was a wholehearted attachment to the ideals of democracy and independence and a fierce devotion to the Allied cause. It came to civil war in the end, but that was not until 1944, in the opening stages of the Cold War.

If I were now addressing a Greek audience I should have expected to be dealing with nautical affairs long before this. The Greek attachment to the sea is as great as the English, and it accounts for a lot of that feeling of closeness that unites two groups of people of otherwise rather different temperaments. The Greek merchant marine was even then of a significant size; it is now among the world's largest. It was at the disposal of the British, and later of the other allies, from the beginning of Greek belligerence. The Hellenic navy, largely of destroyers and submarines, continued to serve in the Mediterranean. They supported, for instance, the Allied landings in Sicily and were there to represent Greece at the Italian surrender in September 1943. It was a proud moment and a fitting revenge for the *Helli*, treacherously sunk just three years earlier.

Besides those who took to the mountains, many Greeks who wanted to continue the struggle left the country. Most of them made their way to the Middle East and especially to Egypt. There they joined the units already being raised from the large and long-established Greek colony. By the autumn of 1942 their numbers had grown to the size of a brigade that, as the 1st Greek Infantry Brigade Group, fought in the Battle of El Alamein as part of the British 50th Division. After reorganization and re-equipment, the Greek force, now renamed 3rd Greek Mountain Brigade, moved to Italy at the end of August 1944. It there became part of the 2nd New Zealand Division, a happy revival of an old association. In the Eighth Army's assault on the German Apennine position, the brigade was actively engaged on the extreme eastern flank and contributed the capture of Rimini to the successful advance in this sector.[15] It was fitting that this fine formation should return to its liberated mother country after winning new triumphs in a field where no Greek troops had fought since Narses, the sixth-century Byzantine commander, had led Justinian's army to capture the city of Rimini from the Goths.

My purpose has been to recall the contribution of the Greeks to the great struggle. It showed great courage to take up the sword at a time when a dark cloud had fallen over Europe. The infectious example brought fresh hope to the oppressed. To Britain, which in that solitary winter of 1940 was suffering both physically and spiritually, it was a gleam of light to feel that they had a new comrade and ally. No one was prepared for the triumphs that were to follow, but all who loved free institutions and the free life of the spirit rejoiced at the worthiness of the gesture. Like Hamlet, who in a flash recovers his sense of purpose and his courage, the Greeks defied augury. They remembered that Hector had declared three millennia beforehand that the only omen worth caring for was to fight for one's country.

NOTES

1. Most notably, those members of the Communist Party of Greece (KKE) who followed the official Kremlin line. These supported the Italians, to maintain the Soviet-Axis alliance. They were few and confused because Metaxas's interior minister, an ingenious Cretan called Maniadakis, had created a bogus KKE, complete with an executive committee and a party newspaper of the

same name as the genuine one. This deception plan deceived even the Stalinist leader, Zachariades. See Tony Judt, *Resistance and Revolution in Mediterraneun Europe 1939–1968* (Oxford: Oxford University Press, 1989), pp. 163ff.

2. The cruiser that bombarded the ancient Venetian citadel in which refugees were housed, killing sixteen Armenian children, was the *San Giorgio*. The next exploit credited to the guns of this warship was in June 1940, when they shot down an aircraft carrying Marshal Italo Balbo, governor of Libya. The latter success was due to a misunderstanding. H. Nicolson, *Curzon, the Last Phase* (London, 1934), p. 368; Ciano, *Diario* (Milan, 1980), p. 447.

3. I.S.O. Playfair, *The Mediterranean and Middle East*. Vol. I (London: HMSO, 1954), p. 25.

4. Macgregor Knox, *Mussolini Unleashed 1939–1941* (Cambridge, 1982), p. 167.

5. Ciano, *op. cit.* p. 458 (17/8/40).

6. *Ibid.*, pp. 469–70 (8 and 12/10/40).

7. Knox, *op. cit.* p. 219.

8. For the opposing orders of battle and comparative strength in equipment, see A. Papagos, *The Battle of Greece* (Athens, 1949), pp. 149ff.

9. Ciano, *op. cit.* p. 484 (4/12/40).

10. Playfair, *op. cit.* p. 223.

11. Ugo Cavallero, "Archivio Secreto," *Europe* 2/17/52. I owe this reference to Mark Dragoumis.

12. I. McD. G. Stewart, *The Struggle for Crete* (London: Oxford University Press, 1966).

13. J. M. A. Gwyer, *History of the Second World War: Grand Strategy*. Vol. III Part I (London: HMSO, 1964), p. 72; for earlier discussions on this point, see pp. 52, 68, 69, and 71.

14. C. M. Woodhouse, *The Story of Modern Greece* (London, 1968), p. 246. The date was the night of 25/26 November. It is often said that this demolition interrupted the main supply line of the German-Italian Army in Egypt, always referred to as "Rommel," before the battle of El Alamein. This is an error: over ninety percent of those supplies had always come through Italy, and by the time the Gorgopotamos viaduct fell into the river, "Rommel" had been retreating from El Alamein for over two weeks.

15. Jackson, *The Mediterranean and Middle East*. Vol. IV Part II (London: HMSO, 1954), p. 296.

THE UNITED NATIONS AND THE PROBLEM
OF GREECE AND ITS NEIGHBORS 1946-1951

Sir Edward Peck

DURING THE EVENTFUL postwar years, 1946-1951, the problems of Greece occupied much of the center of the world political stage, before the lime-light shifted (to the relief of Greece and its hard-pressed people) to subsequent conflicts in Korea, the Middle East, Vietnam, and elsewhere. Even before the end of the 1939-1945 World War, the struggle for power inside Greece itself–between, on the one hand, the well-organized Communist Party (KKE), and, on the other, the various nationalist factions united largely only by a desire to keep their country out of Communist hands–had already been through two rounds. The first round, played out in 1943 under cover of the German-Italian occupation, was indecisive. The second round attempted to forestall the Allied liberation forces in 1944. Its failure led to repeated rumors that the *tritos gyros*, the third round, could not be far off. Indeed, in 1946-1948, the KKE, acting both through its guerrilla army, ELAS, and its political front, EAM, both backed by the Communist neighbors to the north, Albania, Yugoslavia, and Bulgaria, did come very close to seizing power from a succession of weak democratically elected Greek governments. The story of how these attempts were thwarted–by the gradually improving effectiveness of the Greek National Army, supported first by the British Policy and Military Missions and then, when these proved insufficient, by the manifestation of the Truman Doctrine in the shape of massive American economic and military aid, and, finally, by the closure of the Yugoslav frontier when the KKE leader Zachariades was unwise enough to pin his faith on Stalin growing disenchanted with the Greek guerrilla movement, rather than on a previously enthusiastic Tito–has been told several times, by C.M. Woodhouse in the closing chapters of his *Struggle for Greece (1941-49)*, by George Kousoulas in *Revolution and Defeat: The Story of the Greek*

127

Communist Party, and by Edgar O'Ballance in *The Greek Civil War, 1944–1949.*

In his analysis of the causes of the defeat of the Communist guerrillas, O'Ballance concludes that the principal factor was the growing effectiveness of the Greek government's counter-insurgency measures, particularly when the Communists abandoned guerrilla methods for positional warfare, the political leader Zachariades having ousted the guerrilla general Markos Vafiades. O'Ballance maintains that even if the Yugoslav frontier had remained open or, if other factors had worked in their favor, the civil war, though lasting a little longer, would still have ended in defeat for the KKE. In the present writer's view, O'Ballance does not give enough weight to the courage of the Greek people and their growing determination to reject any form of Communist domination or to the increasing political awareness and effectiveness of the Greek authorities. In an earlier chapter, O'Ballance briefly mentions the setting-up of the United Nations Special Committee on the Balkans (UNSCOB), only to dismiss its activities as "ineffectually hovering near the scene of strife in Greece, occasionally issuing a report." The objective of the present article is to examine the part played by the United Nations, not only through the activity of UNSCOB in the years 1948 to 1950, but more particularly the work of its predecessor and parent, the United Nations Special Commission of Investigation concerning Greek Frontier Incidents of 1947, in which the present writer played a modest part. Achievements of the United Nations are at the best of times difficult to assess, but with the merit of hindsight it becomes clear that the Investigation Commission did focus international attention on the trans-frontier support given by Albania, Bulgaria, and Yugoslavia to the Greek Communist guerrillas, and that it did counter Soviet efforts to induce the withdrawal of first British and then United States forces from a weak and relatively defenseless Greece. Moreover, the subsequent Observer Mission (UNSCOB) did fulfil a useful watchdog role, even if it received no cooperation from the three northern neighbors of Greece, while it is true that complete defeat of the guerrillas could only be achieved by the Greek national forces backed by American and, to a lesser degree, British military advice and assistance.

This is not the place to discuss how far the Yalta agreements did in fact lay down a division of spheres of influence in the Balkans between the Western interest in Greece and the Soviet interest in the Balkan states to the north, beyond noting that as early as 21 January 1946 the Soviet

Union, through its representative in the United Nations, brought before the Security Council the charge that the presence of British troops in Greece constituted a threat to peace and security. If the Yalta "fifty-fifty" division was valid, the Soviet Union was already setting about dishonoring it, promoting the interests of the Greek Communists as a means of pushing the Soviet sphere of influence forward to the Mediterranean. That Soviet satellite, the Ukraine, then a member of the Security Council, brought a further charge on 24 August 1946 that the policy of the Greek government had produced a situation in the Balkans endangering international peace and security. Both these charges were rejected in discussion by the Security Council. This United Nations body did, however, consider a request by Greece put forward on 3 December 1946 to give early consideration to a situation leading to friction between Greece on the one hand and Albania, Bulgaria, and Yugoslavia on the other. The Greek government put forward the charge that the guerrilla movement in Greece was recruiting support from the three northern neighbors, that groups of men were being trained for guerrilla activities, and that foreign assistance had been given to them. This charge was supported by a detailed memorandum recounting the numerous guerrilla attacks on villages in northern Greece that had taken place during 1946.

Ten major operations had been carried out by the Greek National Army (GNA), all in Macedonia or Thrace, in the course of that year. The rebels had the advantage of initiative and greater experience of mountain warfare, while the GNA was still inadequately equipped and led—a situation that would persist throughout 1947 and into 1948. The Athens Communist newspaper (which continued to operate freely though in Protean fashion with changes of name) aimed to show the movement as nation-wide, and to play down involvement in the north, particularly after the Security Council, having discussed the Greek complaint as a matter of urgency, resolved on 19 December 1946 to send a commission of investigation "to ascertain the facts relating to the alleged border violations along the frontier between Greece on the one hand and Albania, Bulgaria and Yugoslavia on the other." The Commission was authorized "to conduct its investigation in northern Greece, and in such places in other parts of Greece as the Commission considers should be included in its investigation"; it could also call upon the governments, officials, and nationals of the four countries for relevant information.

The Soviet Union, well aware of the fragility of the situation in Greece, did not veto this resolution, foreseeing the possibility of stirring up further trouble in Greece with the support of the three neighboring countries— all under Communist governments. The Commission was composed of representatives of each of the eleven states then sitting on the Security Council, namely Australia, Belgium, Brazil, China (Nationalist China, at this date), Colombia, France, Poland, the Soviet Union, the United Kingdom, and the United States. The four parties to the dispute appointed liaison representatives, Albania and Bulgaria, then not yet members of the United Nations, accepting the provisions of the United Nations Charter for the purpose of the dispute. The Commission of Investigation, unlike its successor the Observer Mission, thus included representatives from both the Western democracies and from the Communist countries—a combination that was to have very curious results.

On the appointed date of 15 January 1947, the Commission started its work in Athens, where, making good use of its freedom under the democratic constitution of Greece, EAM, the political front of the Communist party, was in full cry both against the continued presence of British forces and against the repressive measures (including the detention of numerous Communist supporters and sympathizers, some of whom were condemned to death) that the Greek authorities found it necessary to impose in their attempt to put down the rebellion. The Commission was thus at once the focus of petitions from EAM and other left-wing organizations to stop the execution of prisoners and the center of a mass demonstration by five thousand EAM supporters. All this activity was grist to the propaganda mill of the Soviet delegate, A. A. Lavrischev (previously Soviet High Commissioner in Bulgaria), who no doubt felt justified in thinking that the Greek government was a ripe plum ready to fall in a few weeks. Indeed, the acquisition of Greece as a member of the Communist camp (thus providing access to the Mediterranean) would have suited his master, Stalin, particularly after Turkey's refusal the previous year to give way to Soviet pressure over the Straits. Even if this view were over-optimistic, the EAM activity lent support to the Communist thesis that it was the mismanagement of the Greek government, not the support from the north, that was the origin of the troubles. Once the basic statements of the four liaison representatives had been heard, the work of the Commission clearly lay in the north of Greece, but the extreme reluctance of Lavrischev to move to Salonika caused the

Commission to remain in Athens for over a month, holding thirty-two meetings there. The United States delegate, Mark Ethridge, editor of the *Louisville Courier*, reported on 17 February that the "highly desirable objective" (of a move to Salonika) was "attained only after Soviets and Poles helped by their satellite liaison officers had exhausted every means of stalling." Unrelenting pressure and the threat of a vote in the Commission by Ethridge and the British delegate, Richard Windle (who, as Chief National Agent of the Labour Party, had been the organizer behind his party's landslide victory in the British elections of 1945), had in fact brought Lavrischev, at 2 A.M., to make the astonishing admission "I give in, I always give in!"

From 25 February to 22 March 1947 the Commission was based on Salonika, holding twenty-nine meetings there, interviewing a selection of the many witnesses presented by the Greek liaison representative, and despatching its field investigating teams to make some thirty-three field investigations on the northern frontiers of Greece, in various parts of the four countries, and on certain Greek islands. Similar procedures, but much curtailed in time owing to the reluctance of the Bulgarian and Yugoslav authorities to admit investigations on their territory, were followed in Sofia on 25 and 26 March, and in Belgrade between 30 March and 2 April. The Commission then proceeded to Geneva to compile its report to the Security Council which was completed on 23 May 1947.

The specific issues before the Commission were three Greek accusations that Albania, Bulgaria, and Yugoslavia (a) supported the guerrilla movement in Greece; (b) interfered in the internal affairs of Greece, aiming at detaching from Greece parts of its territories ("Aegean Macedonia" and "Western Thrace"); and (c) provoked border incidents. The distorting mirror images of these charges were claims by Albania, Bulgaria, and Yugoslavia that the "Greek regime" (a) was responsible for a state of civil war in Greece and the disturbances in the northern districts of Greece; (b) conducted a policy of provocation against its northern neighbors by maintaining in Greek territory war criminals and quislings of those countries and by encouraging subversive activities; and (c) conducted an expansionist foreign policy against its northern neighbors.

The territorial charges and counter-charges were discussed by the Commission from time to time on the basis of statements by the liaison representatives. It was clearly to the advantage of the northern neighbors to make use of the Greek claim to the southern part of Albania (Northern-

Epirus), and of certain Greek proposals for the rectification of the Greco-Bulgarian frontier, to cover up both the Yugoslav objective of annexing Aegean Macedonia and the bare-faced Bulgarian claim to Western Thrace, which it had occupied under the Germans. The Greek liaison representative demonstrated to the Commission that the Greek armed forces were heavily outnumbered by the armies of its northern neighbors, and stated that any frontier adjustments by Greece could and would only be by peaceful means. The territorial issues, though running like a thread through much of the Commission's deliberations, were never live ones, more especially because EAM was in no position to be thought to be giving away pieces of Greek territory. In its final proposals the Commission could do no more than recommend the establishment of good-neighborly relations, and the eventual conclusion of new frontier conventions—an objective that in fact took some fifteen years to achieve.

Similarly, the charges about the activities of refugees were not a major concern of the Commission, though they were investigated. Three field teams visited places of detention in Greece, including the islands of Syros and Ikaria, where some of the twelve-hundred-odd political refugees from Albania, Bulgaria, and Yugoslavia were held: they found no convincing evidence that these alleged "quislings" were being given special treatment or that they were being armed or organized for carrying out activities against the northern neighbors. On 2 April 1947 a team investigated the large camp for Greek refugees in Yugoslavia at Bulkes, northwest of Belgrade, which the Greek authorities asserted was a training camp for guerrillas. The team found no traces of military activity or training, but in the light of statements by twelve witnesses in Greece that they had received training at Bulkes, and other evidence that political indoctrination was carried out there, there is little doubt that matters were "arranged" for the team's visit. Even the French journalist Dominique Eudes maintains in his book *Les Capetanios* that Bulkes was a holding camp, where non-combatants were kept under control in conditions of a miniature police state, but where combatants were selected for military training that in fact took place under General Markos at camps much nearer, or possibly even over, the Greek border.

Despite these diversionary tactics, the Commission was able to devote a good portion of its time to its major task, that is the full investigation of the principal Greek charge that Communist guerrillas active inside Greece were receiving training, hospital facilities, arms and ammunition, and general support from Albania, Bulgaria, and Yugoslavia, and that these countries provided a place of refuge for the guerrillas. Despite vociferous counter-charges, reluctant cooperation, and disingenuous, often unscrupulous, attempts to shake the credibility of witnesses on the part of the Albanian, Bulgarian, and Yugoslav liaison officers, as well as the strong tacit support lent to these maneuvers by the Soviet and, to a lesser extent, the Polish delegates on the Commission, the factual basis of the Greek government's accusations was brought home to the remaining members of the Commission, in particular to those delegates such as the Brazilian, the Colombian, and the Syrian, who were, at the outset, inclined to take a neutral view of the dispute.

Although the charges were denied by the northern governments, there was a substantial basis of evidence in support of the Greek charges that Albania, Bulgaria, and Yugoslavia were actively supporting the guerrilla movement in Greece. For instance, seven witnesses testified that Albania had provided guerrillas with weapons and supplies, seven other witnesses stated that Bulgaria had provided supplies, and seventeen declared that Yugoslavia had done likewise. Similar testimony was given to the effect that guerrillas had been given refuge across the borders, that hospital facilities had been provided, and that guerrilla detachments had been despatched across the northern frontiers into Greece. One particularly damning testimony, which the Soviet delegate went to pains to discredit with allegations of "torture," was that of one Valtadoros, a Greek Communist sympathizer, who sought refuge in Yugoslavia in 1945, who was in the following year despatched back to Greece with an escort of Yugoslav soldiers, and who, after a clash, surrendered to the Greek authorities.

On 18 and 19 March 1947 the Commission itself made on-the-spot investigations of two major incidents that had occurred in 1946 on the Greek-Yugoslav frontier at Skra and Idhomeni. Though the trail was somewhat cold, the lie of the land, the statements of the local inhabitants, and the evidence of the Greek forces were sufficient to convince the nine non-Communist delegates that assistance and refuge had been afforded by Yugoslavia to the guerrillas.

In order to show impartiality, a team, headed by the Belgian delegate, General Delvoie, endeavored between 12 and 15 March to contact Markos Vafiades, the leader of the Communist guerrillas. After waiting for forty-eight hours for Markos to show, the team decided to return to

Salonika: the Soviet and Polish delegates, and also the Albania, Bulgarian, and Yugoslav liaison officers, insisted on remaining to meet the guerrilla "general," who then obligingly appeared and gave them an interview. His statement was later rejected as evidence, not only on the technical ground that it had not been made to a properly constituted team of the Commission, but also, as later transpired, because the question had been put not by any member of the Commission but by a correspondent of the French Communist newspaper, *L'Humanité*.

The Commission had become particularly interested in the 5000-foot ridge of Beles (or Bellashitsa) mountain massif, where the Yugoslav, Bulgarian, and Greek frontiers meet. It was over this ridge that guerrillas had advanced to raid the unfortunate Greek villages of the Doiran plain, retreating to a safe haven when pursued by Greek national forces. In the hope of collecting evidence of this activity on the Yugoslav and Bulgarian side of the mountain, the Commission pressed for a round trip from Doiran in Greece to Strumitsa in Yugoslav Macedonia, returning by Petritch in Bulgaria to Serres in Greece. This tour took place on 16/17 March and, though unproductive of substantive evidence, had a curiously effective impact on those non-Communist members of the Commission who were inclined to doubt the veracity of the Greek charges. For instance, at Strumitsa a large demonstration, patently organized by the Yugoslav authorities, chanted slogans in favor of EAM. Elsewhere witnesses were produced who, when questioned about guerrilla activity, said, like Brer Rabbit, they had "seen nuffin' and heard nuffin'." The present writer recalls an especially telling episode of this kind that took place at the small Bulgarian town of Petritch. Bulgarian witnesses were produced, suitably schooled, to deny the existence of guerrilla activity in of around the town. The Greek liaison officer knew, however, of the Greek-born wife of a local doctor who would have been closely concerned with any medical treatment of wounded guerrillas. The Bulgarian authorities' attempts to obstruct his finding this woman could not be too blatantly deployed in the presence of the Commission and she was, in due course, presented to the Commission for questioning. She appeared at first pleased and proud to appear, and gave ready answers to formal questions about her identity and so on; but when asked what she knew about the presence and hospitalization in Petritch of guerrillas from Greece, her attitude changed abruptly: "These are political questions, which you must not ask me. I cannot answer them." The maverick acting

Australian representative, Sam Atyeo, said that it was clear that the woman was under pressure and demanded ("in the name of the Australian Government") that she be brought to Salonika for questioning under free conditions. This brought Lavrischev to his feet protesting against this infringement of Bulgarian sovereignty. The effect on the doubting Brazilian and Colombian delegates was electric; and Francisco Urrutia (Colombia) became an energetic chairman of the drafting committee and subsequently a convincing rapporteur to the Security Council. In the present writer's view, this episode, unrecorded in the Commission's report, represented a turning-point in the Commission's work.

Similar charades were enacted during the Commissions's short visits to Sofia (26–28 March) and to Belgrade (30 March–2 April) before the Commission departed to Geneva to write its report between 7 April and 23 May, in a quiet atmosphere far removed from the scene of its investigations—and, it may be added, from the possibility of Communist propaganda and demonstrations. On the initiative of Ethridge (United States) and Windle (United Kingdom), and in the face of strong opposition by Lavrischev (Soviet Union), the Commission had attempted to organize a stay-behind group to cover the period while the report was being written in Geneva, but it was only when the matter was taken up in the Security Council in early April that it proved possible to appoint this Subsidiary Group. The Soviet and Polish delegates acquiesced in this decision of the Security Council but the Albanian and Yugoslav liaison representatives refused to cooperate, while the Bulgarian joined it only to delay and obstruct. After the departure of the Commission on 7 April and up to 25 July, the Subsidiary Group managed nonetheless to investigate several incidents on each of the three northern frontiers of Greece, which substantiated the Greek charges of aid to the guerrillas; but, not surprisingly, the Soviet and Polish delegates opposed its conclusions.

The main Commission then set about the not inconsiderable task of reviewing the body of evidence contained in the report of the hearing of 238 witnesses, another 32 statements by organizations, and some 3,000 communications, mainly from EAM. The 20,000 pages of recorded evidence were condensed, under the brisk chairmanship of Francisco Urrutia, to a report that, with appendices, ran to 767 pages. Familiar Soviet tactics such as delay by constant reference to Moscow or the tone of statements, or quibbling over the translation of ambiguous words, soon made it clear that no agreed conclusions would emerge. In fact, the

Commission succeeded in the remarkable achievement of producing in
six weeks a report that, from the same body of evidence, drew diamet-
rically opposed conclusions. Eight of the nine non-Communist delegations, while recognizing the disturbed conditions in Greece in the after-
math of war, noted that nonetheless there was a "considerable degree of
freedom of speech, press and assembly" in Greece, and in particular that
it was only in Greece that witnesses criticized the policies of their own
government. They concluded that, on the basis of the facts ascertained by
the Commission, "Yugoslavia, and to a lesser extent, Albania, and Bulgaria,
have supported the guerilla warfare in Greece." The delegate of France
who, in view of the critical situation of the French government, had
shown considerable apprehension throughout the investigations, ab-
stained from approving these conclusions, on the ground that formal
conclusions were not called for and might inhibit the Commission's task
of pacification and reconciliation. Needless to say, the Soviet and Polish
delegates disagreed totally and submitted a minority set of conclusions,
holding the view that the Greek government was solely responsible for
the conditions in Greece and that the Commission had failed to determine that Albania, Bulgaria, and Yugoslavia were in any way responsible
for provoking or supporting the "civil war in Greece."

The nine non-Communist members, including this time France, submitted proposals to the Security Council to the effect that the four governments concerned should do their utmost to establish good-neighborly
relations, to abstain from all actions likely to increase tension, and to
refrain from overt or covert support of elements in neighboring countries
aiming for the overthrow of the lawful government of those countries;
indeed, future cases of support of armed bands, or a refusal to take
measures to deprive such bands of aid should be considered by the Security Council as a threat to the peace. These proposals, in addition to those
concerning frontier conventions, supervision of refugees, and the voluntary transfer of minorities, included the important one that a body should
be established by the Security Council to investigate future frontier violations, to hear complaints, and, where possible, to use its good offices.
The Soviet and Polish delegates, each using slightly differing arguments,
inevitably rejected these proposals.

The report of the Commission of Investigation regarding Greek Frontier Incidents was laid before the Security Council by Urrutia on 27 June
1947. Members of the Commission were invited to be present in New

York for the debate, which raged long and furiously throughout the summer of 1947. This is no place to recite the detailed arguments made by speakers on both sides: suffice it to say that they followed lines that were familiar to those who had participated in the Commission's discussions. It was inevitable that any resolution to adopt the Commission's proposals would be vetoed by the Soviet delegate, and that veto was in fact cast three times, once on 29 July and twice on 19 August. One result of this inaction was that the Commission and its Subsidiary Group in Greece, which continued to hold meetings (eighty in all) and to report on incidents, both remained in existence.

United Nations' concern at the situation in Greece was not, however, to be stifled in this manner, and later, having pursued the question in the Security Council with the expenditure of a great deal of time and patience only to be met by Soviet vetoes, the American representative on 20 August 1947 asked the Secretary General of the United Nations to place on the agenda of the forthcoming United Nations General Assembly an item entitled "Threats to the political independence and territorial integrity of Greece." It was an item that would remain there for the next four years and, as C. M. Woodhouse observes, the armed struggle which swayed to and fro in the mountains during 1948, to reach deadlock and stalemate, "took second place to the psychological struggle in Greece; and it took third place to the international struggle in Washington and New York, Moscow and London, which began with the Truman Doctrine and had no foreseeable end."[1]

The United Nations General Assembly (UNGA) decided on 23 September 1947 to discuss the question, referred it to the First Committee (Political and Security), and, on 21 October 1947, by 110 votes in favor, 6 against (the Soviet bloc), and 11 abstentions, the UNGA adopted Resolution 109 (II), which created the United Nations Special Committee on the Balkans (to be known as UNSCOB). This resolution, which set the pattern for United Nations resolutions on Greece in subsequent years, took account of the report by the Committee of Investigation, which found that Albania, Bulgaria, and Yugoslavia had given assistance and support to the guerrillas fighting against the Greek government. The resolution called upon the four countries to "establish normal diplomatic and good-neighborly relations"; to establish frontier conventions; to cooperate in the voluntary repatriation of refugees and to "take effective measures to prevent the participation of such refugees in political and

military activity" (this last recommendation was to assume greater importance as the years went by). The four countries were also to "study the
practicability of concluding agreements for the voluntary transfer of
minorities" (this provision remained virtually a dead letter). To observe
the compliance of the four governments with these recommendations,
and to assist them in their implementation, the Assembly resolution set
up the "Special Committee" (that is to say, UNSCOB) to report back at its
next regular session; it consisted of representatives of Australia, Brazil,
China, France, Mexico, Netherlands, Pakistan, the United Kingdom, and
the United States, seats being held open for Poland and the Soviet Union.
(Needless to say, neither of these two states, which had already on 11
October announced that they would not take part in the work of the
Special Committee, ever did take up their seats; this is hardly surprising
after their experience with the Commission of Investigation.) Finally, the
Assembly, aware of the difficulties that had arisen over the Commission
of Investigation's prolonged stay in Athens and of the need for the Special
Commission to be close to the scene of action, insisted that its principal
headquarters should be in Salonika, though it might perform its duties
elsewhere (with the cooperation of the four countries, which was, in
fact, only extended by Greece) as it deemed appropriate.

After some preliminary meetings in Paris and Athens, UNSCOB set up
its headquarters in Salonika on 1 December 1947 and met there until June
1948, when it decided that sittings could, in general, be more conveniently held in Athens. In November 1947 it decided to set up Observation Groups, composed of representatives of seven of the nine countries,
which would tour the northern frontiers of Greece to report continu-
ously to the Committee to what extent good-neighborly relations existed
between Greece and its northern neighbors. The activities of these
Observation Groups were naturally restricted, not only by the refusal of
the Albanian, Yugoslav, and (save in a limited number of formal instances)
Bulgarian authorities to cooperate with UNSCOB, but also even on the
Greek side of the frontier (where the Greek authorities gave full facilities), because of guerrilla control of certain areas and by extensive mining
of roads by guerrillas in the whole frontier area. Nonetheless, in the first
year (up to June 1945) the Observation Groups were able to make fifty-
eight reports, which fully confirmed the continuation of the state of
affairs reported by the Investigation Committee, that is to say; Greek
guerillas were crossing freely from Albania, Bulgaria, and Yugoslavia into

Greece and back again, that there was firing from Albanian and Yugoslav territory into Greece, and that medical and logistical assistance was given by Albania, Bulgaria, and Yugoslavia to Greek guerrillas.

UNSCOB's exhaustive attempts to obtain the cooperation of three of the four governments concerned took up a great deal of time and paper, occupying a large section in its report. Except for the cooperation of the Greek government, which was freely and fully given, these efforts by UNSCOB met with either stony silence, total non-cooperation, or occasional counter-charges, which could not be investigated owing to that very lack of cooperation. Nor did it prove possible to make any progress either on the establishment of normal diplomatic and good-neighborly relations, or on the problems of frontier conventions, refugees, and minorities.

In its reporting of political developments, UNSCOB was more successful. On 24 December 1947 Markos Vafiades proclaimed his Provisional Democratic Government and declared his intention to establish diplomatic relations with the "democratic countries." UNSCOB reacted promptly by issuing on 29 December a strong warning that "recognition even *de facto* of the movement describing itself as the 'Provisional Democratic Greek Government' followed by direct or indirect aid and assistance to an insurrectionary movement against a government of a member of the U.N. in defiance of international law, peace treaties, and the principles of the Charter would constitute a grave threat to the 'maintenance of international peace and security'." It is impossible to establish whether the governments of Albania, Bulgaria, and Yugoslavia were or were not, in fact, inclined to recognize Markos at this date, or whether they were deterred by UNSCOB's warning. But, in any event, they did not recognize the Provisional Democratic Government. Instead, they set up Committees to aid the "Greek Democratic People," which collected money, food, and clothing and engaged in approved propaganda on behalf of the guerrillas. UNSCOB was also successful in locating the "Free Greece" radio station, broadcasting from Yugoslavia, and the monitoring of these broadcasts provided useful (and damning) evidence of continued support for the guerrillas. UNSCOB also tackled the alarming problem of the "removal and retention" of approximately 60,000 Greek children between the ages of three and fourteen, which, the Greek Foreign Minister protested, was more than "a mere violation of treaty pledges," it was "a crime against humanity." There was little doubt of the facts: the "Free

Greece" and Belgrade radios frequently and readily admitted that large numbers of Greek children had arrived in Yugoslavia and were to be distributed to Albania, Czechoslovakia, and Hungary. Although the Communist authorities maintained that the children had been sent away for safety's sake, UNSCOB was able to establish from witnesses that, in a substantial number of cases, children had been forcibly removed or that parents had agreed under duress to the removal of their children. UNSCOB considered that the reception and retention of these children, without their parents' consent, raised the issue of inherent rights of parents, and that their protracted retention would be contrary to accepted moral standards of international conduct. This issue would occupy the United Nations for a number of years, since the Communist indoctrination of these children and their reinfiltration into Greece, often many years later, were to be a cause of trouble to come. So much for the substance of UNSCOB's report of 30 June 1948, which recommended to the UNGA the continuation of the Special Committee's existence.

The UNGA had no hesitation in renewing for another year the mandate of UNSCOB, which reported on similar lines on 2 August 1949. This time, there was an important development to note, for, although the Committee stated that Bulgaria and Albania continued to furnish moral and material assistance to the Greek guerrillas, providing "large quantities of war material," allowing extensive use of their territories, assisting the guerrillas to recruit Greeks in their territories, including sending back adolescent boys and girls to fight in Greece, the Committee considered that similar aid from Yugoslavia in the second half of 1948 had "diminished and may have ceased." The report also noted the transfer of "Free Greece" radio from Yugoslavia to Romania. These developments reflected the noticeable reduction and eventual cessation of Yugoslav interest in fomenting the guerrilla movement in Greece as a result of the rift between Belgrade and Moscow and the ill-judged decision of the KKE leader Zachariades to transfer his allegiance from Tito to Stalin, who had, in any case, by then become disenchanted with the Greek guerrilla movement.[2]

This report by UNSCOB was concluded shortly before the powerful offensive launched in August 1949 by the Greek government forces against the guerrillas on Mount Grammos, up against the Albanian frontier. This well-planned offensive was eminently successful and between 20 August and 2 September 1949 not more than 5,000 rebels, according to the Greek High Command, remained on Greek soil, and this number dwindled rapidly in the following months. UNSCOB saw fit to submit on 19 September 1949 a supplementary report stating that "the Greek Armed Forces have eliminated guerrilla resistance along the northern borders of Greece and have resumed effective control of these areas." It added that a large proportion of the Greek guerrillas and other Greek nationals had "sought refuge in or been forcibly taken into" Albania and Bulgaria, Yugoslavia having closed its frontier with Greece. Though these refugees were said to have been disarmed and interned, UNSCOB reminded Albania and Bulgaria of their duty "to prevent the use of their territory in any way against the security of the Greek state."

Nonetheless, UNSCOB's essential watchdog function continued for another two years and its annual reports reflect a shift for the better in the international situation in the Balkans. The report of 31 July 1950 noted the improved situation along the northern frontiers, commented favorably on Yugoslavia's closure of its frontier with Greece to guerrillas, and considered that the "continuing political threat to Greek political independence and territorial integrity is to be found at present chiefly in Bulgaria." This was not due to any absence of continuing ill-will on the part of Albania, but rather that the withdrawal of Yugoslav support had isolated Albania from direct contact with the other Soviet-controlled countries of the Balkans. UNSCOB did, however, consider that the threat to Greece had "altered in character," in that the organized guerrilla movement within Greece now consisted of the activities of scattered bands, but that the remnants of the movement within Greece had not been dissolved. Moreover, there had been no international verification of the "many thousands" of Greek guerrillas who had fled northwards, so that even though the effort to dominate Greece by armed force had been suspended, the aim of the guerrilla leaders, which was continually proclaimed by the "Free Greece" radio station operating in Romania, had not been abandoned. UNSCOB stressed the need for continued vigilance over the territorial integrity of Greece in the interest of peace and security in the Balkans. And it also viewed "with the gravest concern the fact that no Greek children have yet been repatriated to their homes in Greece" despite two unanimous resolutions of UNGA.

The Special Committee's final report, to the Sixth General Assembly, was signed on 15 August 1951 and released on 16 September. The more optimistic note which crept in as a result of the resumption of diplomatic relations between Greece and Yugoslavia on 28 November 1950, and the consequent cooperation of Yugoslavia with the International Red Cross in the repatriation of children, was tempered by the observation that support propaganda and recruiting for the forcible overthrow of the Greek government centered in Romania had now extended to Poland, Czechoslovakia, and Hungary, where special training schools for guerrillas had been set up. It concluded that the threat to Greece had changed in character and that, although there was no attempt to resume large-scale guerrilla warfare, a "widespread and highly organized network" assisted the infiltration into Greece of small armed groups of "specially selected and trained guerrillas to reorganize the Greek Communist and 'Agrarian' Parties, foment discontent, and generally prepare for the forcible overthrow of the Greek Government." This report was sufficiently encouraged by the improvement in the situation and the capacity of the Greek government to cope with this diminished threat that it did not recommend to the Assembly the continuation of UNSCOB, but simply the maintenance of United Nations vigilance over the Balkans. On 7 December 1951 the Assembly, after expressing its appreciation of UNSCOB's services and of the "difficult and dangerous task" carried out by the observers, decided to discontinue the Special Committee and reassigned its function of continued vigilance to a Balkan sub-commission of the Peace Observation Commission, established under the "Uniting for Peace" resolution.

The problem of outside intervention in Greece, which had been gradually fading from the center of world attention since 1949, was thus removed from the effective agenda of the UNGA, while focus shifted to the events in the Far East, Korea, and Vietnam, which, together with the Middle East, were to occupy the world stage for more than the next twenty years.

In attempting to assess the achievements of the United Nations, in particular of the Investigation Commission and of its successor, the Special Observation Committee (UNSCOB), it is important neither to assess them too highly, nor, as O'Ballance does, to dismiss them altogether. It is also important to place these achievements in the historical context of subsequent United Nations activity elsewhere. On the one hand, it is clear that the Greek forces could not, by their own resources alone, have overcome the Communist guerrillas, and that the substantial American and British assistance was essential in making victory a real possibility. On the other hand, there is no doubt that the report of the Investigation Committee was extremely important in bringing before the United Nations, and, through it, to the world in general, what was going on in northern Greece. Equally, the subsequent reports of the observer groups of UNSCOB kept the Communist intervention in Greece before the eyes of all those members of the United Nations whose minds were not firmly closed on the subject. Without those reports, neither the American administration, nor President Truman, nor the British Labour Government, under the strong partnership of Clement Attlee and Ernest Bevin, would have found it easy to counter, as firmly and as successfully as they did, the propaganda of the vociferous left-wing minorities (particularly in Britain). Nor would they have been on such solid ground for justifying to Congress and to Parliament the support given to the Greek authorities by the American and British Military Missions in logistics, advice, and otherwise.

Moreover, although this United Nations activity and interest, which was spread over four years, did not of itself bring about the cessation of guerrilla activity in Greece, it did set a pattern for subsequent United Nations interventions in Korea, in the Congo, in Palestine, and in Cyprus, which, with varying degrees of success, served in an unspectacular way to maintain some part of the fabric of international peace and security. Certainly the two United Nations bodies concerned with Greece—the Investigation Committee and UNSCOB—were interesting pioneering experiments, which, while posing considerable limitations on United Nations action, were effective in presenting, in as objective a fashion as possible, rather than through the distorting mirror of the press and broadcast media, a critical problem before the eyes of the world, and in keeping it there while substantive action was prepared and executed by those best able to do so.

NOTES

1. C. M. Woodhouse, *The Struggle for Greece 1941–1949* (London, 1976), p. 227.

2. It is an interesting footnote to history that as early as the period of the compilation of the Investigation Commission's report in Geneva April–June 1947 signs of friction between the Soviet and Yugoslav delegations were already apparent, although Western observers on the Commission found them

perplexing at a time when the Soviet Union and Yugoslavia were thought to be acting in concert over Greece. The Yugoslav representative, Josip Djerdja (who subsequently, while Yugoslav minister to Albania, incurred the first overt sign of the Moscow-Belgrade rift), would make long and impassioned statements, sometimes lasting up to three hours, in support of the guerrilla cause; the Soviet representative, speaking briefly in general support of the Yugoslav thesis, could not, to the surprise of Western observers, conceal his evident irritation at Djerdja's behavior.

GREEKS AND JEWS
IN THE SHADOW OF THE HOLOCAUST

Mark Mazower

SEVEN YEARS AGO, when the name of Kurt Waldheim was in every news-paper, I worked for a British TV company, looking in particular into what he had been doing in Greece a little more than half a century ago. Thus started a long period of research, which continued well after the TV program had been made and after Waldheim's name had dropped from the headlines: the result was my book, *Inside Hitler's Greece*, which was published a year and a half ago. In this book I tried to look at the overall impact of German rule on life in Greece—its social, political and economic consequences. I remember that as I was writing the first draft, I met a friend of mine in Oxford. She asked me whether I planned to write about the fate of the Jews. I told her that I couldn't decide. On the one hand, I felt it was important, especially as there was so little on the subject in English. On the other hand, perhaps it was too important to include merely as one chapter in a rather long book that was chiefly concerned with other matters. She told me I had to, and I followed her advice. Perhaps my hesitations reflected a more general uncertainty among historians of modern Greece about how to fit the story of Greece's Jewish population into their analyses. Had I left that chapter out, I would have been following in a long tradition of writers for whom more or less all that mattered in recent Greek history was the struggle between Left and Right. The three years—1941 to 1944—of German occupation, with their story of dreadful famine, social disintegration, mass resistance, and Nazi reprisal had come to be seen, more or less, as a prelude to the Civil War between Communist rebels and royalists that ravaged the country at the end of the 1940s.

Today, of course, we hardly need to be persuaded of the importance of ethnic and religious minorities in European history. Greece's Jewish

communities may not have been large but they included both some of the
most ancient in Europe—the so-called Romaniote congregations in
central Greece and the islands—as well as the illustrious, proud, and
powerful Sefardic city of Salonika, the "Mother of Israel." Recently there
has been a resurgence of interest in the history of these communities—
overdue perhaps, very welcome nonetheless. We now have a splendid
Jewish Museum in Athens, an energetic Society for Greek-Jewish Studies
in Salonika, and the scholarly *Bulletin of Judaeo-Greek Studies* from
Cambridge.

Each time I visit the bookshops here or in Athens I am struck by the
quantity of new work being produced on this subject, ranging from
photo albums, books of Greek-Jewish cuisine to guides to the surviving
synagogues of Greece and, of course, survivors' memoirs. I would like to
contribute to this process of rediscovery by describing to you the Final
Solution in Greece through the eyes of an historian. What parts of this
tragic story can we reconstruct from the archives, and what still remains
to be recovered? How, too, can the story of the fate of Greek Jewry
contribute more generally to our understanding of this terrible period in
European history?

Let me begin with an article in *Die Zeit* from March 9, 1997. Here is
reported the astonishing news that the archives of the Jewish community
of Salonika have been discovered in Russia and are now in the possession
of the Russian Federation's Commission for Archival Affairs. How did
they get there? At the very start of the Nazi occupation of Greece, in the
spring of 1941, the chief ideologue of the Third Reich, Alfred Rosenberg,
sent a special unit—the so-called Sonderkommando Rosenberg—of academics, bibliographers, and army officers to visit and report on the Jewish
communities, the small chiefly Greek-speaking congregations of Athens,
Crete, Corfu, Volos, as well as the fifty-thousand strong Ladino-speaking
population of northern Greece. They stayed for six months, and in that
time they carried out their work with exemplary thoroughness. Their
mission was not, of course, merely to visit these communities; it was also
to ransack them of their valuables—libraries, precious manuscripts, religious objects—all of which were to be taken back to enrich Rosenberg's
dream of a new research institute that he planned to set up in Frankfurt.
In 1943, the director of the new Library for the Study of the Jewish Ques-

tion boasted that among the 500,000 volumes in his collection were some 10,000 books and manuscripts from Greece. "In the New Order of European organization," he added, "the Library for the Jewish Question, not only in Europe but in the entire world, will be here in Frankfurt." Well, things worked out slightly differently. For years it was believed that the plunder from Greece had been destroyed by bombing in Germany itself; now it transpires that it survived only to be seized by the Red Army and brought to Moscow.

As it turned out, the activities of the Rosenberg unit were the first and last unified action to be carried out by the Germans against the Jews of Greece. In 1941, the Axis powers had carved the country up into zones: the Italians, with central and southern Greece, took most of the territory; the Germans, holding on to Salonika and its hinterland, most of the Jews. Then, on 11 July 1942, Eichmann's office in the RSHA wrote a long memorandum to the Foreign Ministry entitled "Handling of the Jewish Question Abroad" [Behandlung der Judenfrage im Ausland]. It talked about the "preparation for the Final Solution of the European Jewish Question" and suggested several measures to be taken against the Jews in Greece—notably the wearing of a star and the internment of German Jewish refugees—while the Foreign Office persuaded the Italians in their zone to cooperate. However, as Jonathan Steinberg has now shown us, the Italians refused this cooperation, forcing the SS to proceed alone with the *Judenverfolgung* in northern Greece at the beginning of 1943.

The SS were not entirely alone, of course, for both the Wehrmacht and the Foreign Ministry were cooperating fully. The Foreign Ministry had its own Jewish affairs desk, which had been receiving information since 1938 about Salonika's community from their consul in the city; as for the Wehrmacht, it was none other than General von Krenzski, the area commander, who had initiated the first major action against the city's Jews, when he ordered the humiliation and mass registration of adult males in the summer of 1942 and put them to work building roads and airstrips. Few of us are likely now to be persuaded by von Krenzski's postwar defense that he had been motivated not by hatred of the Jews but by concern at the poor roads in his area.[1]

Without doubt the key figure in the Salonika deportations was the infamous Dieter Wisliceny, portrayed in Errikos Sevillias's memoirs as "at first sight looking like a schoolteacher or clerk, especially when in civilian dress, but violent and aggressive when angry." The sturdy Wisliceny was the man chosen by Eichmann to supervise the deportations from Salonika. Not only was he an old friend; he was also one of the RSHA's chief "experts" in the Jewish question. We have a good idea of what a man in his position knew about high-level intentions towards the Jews thanks to the detailed answers he gave to Allied war crimes investigators at Nuremberg in 1945.

In the unpublished transcripts of Wisliceny's interrogation, now held at the Imperial War Museum in London, we can read not only about his activities in Slovakia and Greece, but also about the way in which he found out the true nature of the business he was involved in.

In June 1942, so he said, he had visited Eichmann in Berlin. Eichmann had opened a safe in his office and taken out an order from Himmler that indicated that "the Führer had ordered the final solution of the Jewish question." When Wisliceny asked what this meant, Eichmann told him that the expression "final solution" really meant "the biological annihilation of all Jews." Hence by the time, some eight months later, that he arrived in Salonika, Wisliceny could have had no doubt about the ultimate purpose of his mission.

He arrived there in early February and worked with enormous speed. It seems now almost incredible that almost 50,000 people could have been controlled so easily and so swiftly. Yet by late March the deportations to Auschwitz were under way. Thousands of Jews had been herded into the Baron Hirsch camp—a newly created transit center by the railway station—and sent northwards.

The role of the Jewish communal leadership in the city has not escaped controversy. Chief Rabbi Koretz, in particular, was accused after the war of having worked too closely, perhaps even of having collaborating, with the Occupation authorities.

I am inclined to doubt this charge, which mirrors similar accusations leveled at other leaders operating elsewhere in Europe in similar circumstances. Koretz, it is true, was a headstrong man in a terrifying predicament who had made a perhaps premature decision that resistance would be useless.

But what documentary evidence there is suggests that far from collaborating, he was prepared to go behind the backs of the Germans and make what efforts he could—at some personal risk—to have the deportations halted.

What documentary evidence there is .... The basic problem for any historian of the Final Solution is that the files of the main body responsible, the RSHA, do not—so far as we know—survive. But a little detective work allows some gaps to be filled in, and here is an example. On 15 April 1943, we gain a glimpse from the German Foreign Ministry records of what Rabbi Koretz had been trying to do: on that day, an angry Wisliceny reported both to the Army commander for the Salonika area and to Consul Schonberg that he had just interrogated Koretz.

Koretz had desperately attempted to enlist Prime Minister Rallis's support in his efforts to halt the deportations. According to Wisliceny's account, the rabbi had managed to gain an interview with Rallis on 11 April, but at the crucial moment "his nerves gave way, and weeping he could only beg that Rallis intervene with the German authorities so that the *Kultusgemeinde* that had existed for 2,000 years in Salonika would not be liquidated. The Prime Minister gave a brief inconsequential reply." Did this [K's] account correspond to the facts? Wisliceny himself thought so. So did consul Schonberg, who commented to his superior that another witness to this meeting had told him that Rallis had been "visibly shaken" and had answered the rabbi that "it was not in his power to stop the deportation of the Jews. He could only make recommendations to the occupation authorities." As a result of trying to hinder a military order, Koretz and his family were placed under house arrest by order of the Bfh Sal./Aegais before being deported to Bergen-Belsen.[2]

Let me just mention at this point that Waldheim himself almost certainly had nothing to do with the deportations since they were not the responsibility of military intelligence, which was where he worked. The Wehrmacht's civilian administrator in Salonika, Max Merten, Eichmann's SS operatives trike [Wisliceny] and German consul-general Schonberg— these were the people in the city chiefly responsible for what was happening. On the other hand, Waldheim is obviously lying when he says he knew nothing of what was happening. The sudden removal of tens of thousands of people set in train a series of social, political and economic problems and possibilities that no one could ignore.

What, for instance, was to happen to the properties and possessions they left behind? This concern looms large in the testimonies and recollections of that time:

> "The piano we gave to a neighbour who promised to look after it, together with the carpets we gave him," writes Erika Counio in her

moving memoir. "He promised to return it as soon as we got back. The photographer Malanides, a close friend of my father's, agreed to keep an eye on the drawing room with the beautiful carved bookcase full of books of my parents, the office with its beautiful oak table. My grand-mother's and my mother's jewels we gave to another very good friend."[3]

Or from Nikos Kokantzis's fine autobiographical novella of wartime Salonika, *Gioconda*, this description of the final parting between his family and his Jewish neighbors:

> Then came the moment when they could no longer pretend there was anything more to get ready. Everything was done. We all stood there in helpless silence. Madam Leonora went round all the rooms closing the shutters and closing the windows. Very carefully. The house grew dark. From above her dressing-table in their bedroom she took an old oblong box made of brown leather and gave it to my mother. "Please do me a favour and look after this? I've some jewelry inside which I wouldn't want to fall into the wrong hands. There's a brooch of my mother's, and one of the rings belonged to my grandmother. Will you take them? For the children, at least ... And ... if we decide not to come back to Greece, when it is all over, if it suits us better to stay there ... you know ... then keep them for yourself to remember us by. Will you?" "But of course ... My God, yes, of course." My mother's voice was barely audible and her hands were shaking.[4]

Unlike novelists and memoirists, historians of the Final Solution have had little—till now—to say about this sensitive subject. But we are in a posi-tion to make certain observations about the case of Salonika. In the spring of 1988, I called upon the late Joseph Lovinger in Athens, then president of the Central Board of Jewish Communities, to ask whether he had any documents that bore upon the Waldheim affair. No, he said, but was I interested in some files that had just been delivered to his office from the cellars of the Ministry of Justice? He had not had time to look at them yet, but ... Upstairs he showed me four large jute sacks, unopened and filthy with a dirt that suggested they had been left abandoned for decades. I opened one at random. Papers in complete disorder; thousands of docu-ments had just been stuffed in at random. What were they? I began to read:

9 October 1943

> To the relevant committee for the disposal of Jewish properties via the Popular Committee for Refugees from the District of Drama:

> I hereby have the honour to inform you that as a refugee from the village of X ... and finding myself here without property or work, I beg you to do whatever may be necessary to make me trustee of an equivalent property from those Jewish ones at your disposal for my professional use and shelter.

> I additionally confirm that I have brought no goods or tools with me here. All the above I declare in full knowledge of the penalties imposed by the Law on perjury. With respect, yours—etc.

There were hundreds of such requests from Greek refugees from the Bulgarian zone for a shop or workshop; requisition orders from the German military or SS; the accounts, often stretching back years before the war, of Jewish firms. In all, these seemed to be the files of an organization called YDIP [the Service for the Disposal of Israelite Property]. At random, I selected a number of the more obviously important documents: one was the catalogue of Jewish properties—some 1800 entries—drawn up by the community itself on German orders—upon which YDIP based its work. The others included some of the minutes of the Board of Directors, dating from the spring of 1943 onwards. The writing was by now badly faded and sometimes indecipherable. But enough survived to enable me to determine the bare bones of what had happened.

Occupation Law 205, published by the Athens Government at the end of May 1943 but agreed to at the very beginning of the Rallis Government in April, had established YDIP as a body run by civil servants, local businessmen, and other Greek notables. Although Law 205 had made no reference to the occupation authorities, in practice, of course, YDIP was subordinate to them. While some of the Greek directors had wanted to use the properties to help house Greek refugees from the Bulgarian zone, others, of course, simply acted as patrons for friends and relatives, while the local Army and SS sought to obtain favors for collaborators and informers.

Ilias Douros, who ran YDIP, was a former manager of the National Mortgage Bank. He seems to have taken a very literal view of his responsibilities, i.e., finding "caretakers" rather than new owners for the 1800 premises. But his problems seemed endless—one ends up almost feeling sorry for him. In the first place, he complains that he cannot value the premises and their stocks correctly. They are being looted day and night, even by the policemen and soldiers deputed to guard them, not to mention by his employees. Public order in the deserted streets has totally broken down; at night there are shoot-outs. Then there is the question of German interference: both Dr. Max Merten from the Wehrmacht and the SiPo/SD are constantly telling him to hand over properties to their nominees. Hardly any has he managed to hand over in a regular fashion. When he protests at the low character of the beneficiaries of German generosity, a SiPo official waves a revolver in his face. In the summer of 1943 he tries to resign. He is told to stay where he is.

YDIP was, of course, not unique. The Second World War witnessed an enormous transfer of wealth and property across the continent effected through inflation, coercion and force, and often legitimated by a thin veneer of legality. What happened to Europe's Jews formed part of this process, nasty but important for understanding the new social and economic configurations that emerged out of the war. The paucity of documentary evidence makes it difficult to gauge how all this struck people at the time. The relevant official Greek archives are closed; the Germans make no reference to such matters. The Italians were out of the war by then, and all foreign consulates in the city had been shut down. Luckily for us, however, the Americans had secret contacts in the Greek Ministry of the Interior in Athens. Thus, we find in Washington, in the archives of the OSS, a memorandum written by a Greek civil servant who had visited Salonika a few months after the deportations had finished. According to him, the treatment of Jewish property was "scandalous and alarming." Few bona fide refugees from the Bulgarian zone had been housed; indeed, many Jewish apartments had been demolished either because they had been so badly plundered or because they had been taken apart by people looking for valuables [rumors]. "My personal impressions of the general treatment of this stupendous problem are sorrowful," he wrote.

Control of Jewish property and possessions—to put it bluntly, money and extortion—remained at the center of German concerns when their attention switched later in 1943 from Salonika to Athens. The Italian collapse that September brought the former Italian zone, including Athens and the islands, under direct German control. This put the tiny but ancient communities of central Greece and the islands as well as Athens itself, where hundreds of Salonikan Jews had taken refuge, in terrible danger. Almost immediately Eichmann started planning a second round of deportations. But we now know—from the Foreign Ministry files together with several other sources—that these did not run nearly as smoothly as Eichmann would have wished. Jurgen Stroop, who left the ruins of the Warsaw Ghetto to become the SS chief in Athens for a short period that autumn, botched the whole business badly, allowing Elias Barxilai, the Chief Rabbi of the capital, to escape hidden in a mail van into the hills with the assistance of the Greek resistance movement EAM/ELAS. Stroop was recalled to Germany under a cloud. In October, Prime Minister Rallis informed the German Foreign Ministry of his strong opposition to the deportations—perhaps in this way his painful interview with Koretz in April had had some effect. In a letter dated 7 October, he praised the loyalty of the "Jewish community of Old Greece" and the anxiety felt "both by the Greek state and by every Greek heart" at the proposed deportations of "these Greek citizens from their homeland." I shall come later to the significance of the distinction apparently being drawn here between the Romaniote Greek-speaking Jews of Athens and the islands and the Ladino communities to the north.[5]

Rallis's letter was reinforced—quite fortuitously—by events occurring hundreds of miles away in Denmark. There, the Gestapo's decision to arrest and deport the country's small Jewish population precipitate a major political and military crisis. The result of this was that the German Foreign Ministry managed to persuade a reluctant SS in Berlin to postpone the planned deportations from Greece. In the meantime, the SiPo/SD office in Athens extended its control over the property of those Jews who had gone underground. The Foreign Ministry had proposed letting the Greek state handle this, as had happened in Salonika; but security police chief Walter Blume had successfully blocked the idea. In Athens—as later on the Ionian and Dodecanese islands—Blume's men thus collected funds with which to enrich both themselves and their agents.

Who were these men—commonly but erroneously identified as belonging to the "Gestapo"? Throughout the postwar period, the [West] German Justice Ministry has been investigating Nazi war crimes. Although few investigations result in trials and still fewer in convictions, the admirable investigating lawyers in their War Crimes Office at Ludwigsburg have succeeded in collecting an enormous quantity of material.

I came across this more or less by chance. My original purpose in visiting Ludwigsburg was to look at some files from the Greek War Crimes Office, which needless to say were unavailable in Greece. What I found was perhaps more important—among other things, detailed investigations into the activities of Verwaltungsrat Dr. Max Merten in

Salonika and Standartenführer Dr. Walter Blume in Athens. Postwar inter-
views with these men and with many of their colleagues provided an
indispensable source for understanding how the Final Solution took
place in Greece, and what sort of men were responsible. Some—like the
sadistic Toni Burger—clearly enjoyed the opportunities for killing that
went with their job. Some, like the driver of one of the trucks that drove
the Jews of Jannina that cold, snowy morning in March 1944 across the
Katara pass to the train and Auschwitz, were lowly soldiers who, after the
war, became factory workers, street cleaners—"little men" as they described themselves. Others were cold-blooded, ambitious bureaucrats.
Walter Blume—as Security Police Chief, the most important SS figure in
Athens in the last year of the war—was a well-trained lawyer. He had
already killed hundreds of innocent people as commander of a death
squad in Russia in the summer of 1941 before being recalled because of
his reluctance to kill women and children.

In my opinion, the various archives I have described to you do now
permit us to reconstruct much of what happened from the German end:
in the Bundesarchiv in Koblenz we can find the very first wartime report
on Greek Jews, written in November 1941 by the head of the Sonderkommando Rosenberg after six months investigation, and running to more
than fifty pages. It is this report that, memorably observes—with some
disappointment—that "for the average Greek there is no Jewish question." From Bonn, we find the rather ill-tempered memo dating from
October 1944 in which a Foreign Ministry accountant tries to sort out
who should foot the bill for the *Judentransporten* from Greece. As to
what happened in between, we can piece this together in the fashion I
have described.

What remains much less clear is something I have already alluded to,
the range of reactions and responses in Greece itself during and after the
events of 1943–44. The fifty-year rule, in theory, should allow research-
ers in Greece access to official files for this period. In theory. In practice,
of course, the situation is less favorable. Why indeed should we expect
the Greek state to release what could be rather compromising material

He survived the war and the Nuremberg trials, staying in prison for a
few years. When he was released, he remarried and adopted four children. He died in 1971, investigated but never put on trial for his part in
the Final Solution or the mass executions that swept Athens in the last
year of the war.

when it is so reluctant to release much more mundane files, or indeed to organize its whole public records system on a properly professional basis?

At present we can only ask questions, and then look for other, mostly non-official, Greek sources to help us answer them. Take, for example, a small item in a wartime newspaper. *The Larissaikos Typos*—a provincial paper from the Italian zone—on 4 April 1943 reported a new German decree prohibiting Greek Orthodox families on pain of death from adopting Jewish babies, and offering an amnesty to those who gave them up. How widespread this practice was we cannot as yet say. Clearly even in the spring of 1943 there was much sympathy shown to Jews by their Christian neighbors, reinforced no doubt by the teachings of the Church leadership. The records of orphanages—some held in the Jewish Museum in Athens—shed further light on these numerous stories of generosity and tragedy. We know, for example, of the many efforts made by Archbishop Damaskinos, the wartime head of the Orthodox Church in Athens, to intervene with the German authorities. Let me refer to two specific instances: on 31 March 1944, in other words, after the Jews had been interned in Haidari but before they had been sent northwards to Auschwitz, Damaskinos appealed to the Germans to exempt "the young, the elderly, war invalids and victims" from deportation. He was told that orders from Berlin forbade exceptions under any circumstances.

On 5 April, Damaskinos tried again, this time on behalf of a Jewish woman who had married an Orthodox Greek, Joannis Dimakis. She and their two children had been deported. A handwritten note in the German file stated briefly "Special treatment unavoidable [Sonderbehandlung unvermeidlich]." Anyone familiar with the language of the Third Reich will know how to interpret that phrase.

Of course, there was also a darker side: as everywhere there were people who sought to profit from the misfortune of others. Some were creatures of the SS—like members of the extremist Poulos organization—who sold off Jewish properties to finance their murderous activities. Others were—how can one describe them?—professional anti-Semites who would have liked to gain German favor. There were simple gangsters, who saw the vulnerable Jews as an opportunity to get rich quick.

And, of course, there were all those who in one way or another had benefited from the Jews' departure. According to information from December 1944 about 1,000 Jewish families were unable to return to their homes because these were occupied by new tenants.

The position did not immediately improve: two letters from January 1945 talk of an "anti-Jewish movement on a considerable scale developing in the towns" chiefly among "those shop-owners who 'inherited' Jewish shops and people who have taken over the houses of which the Jews were robbed during the Nazi occupation." The postwar law of return of property was not at first applied outside Athens, while several hundred survivors were—irony of ironies—caught by another law confiscating the property of enemy subjects.[6]

This information comes from bulletins of the Jewish Agency for Palestine. How accurate it was it is hard to say. Obviously, the Agency had an interest in making life in Europe sound as unattractive for Jews as possible. But then that was not difficult in 1945. My own impression is that in a comparative perspective Greece stands out for the extent of the support lent by Christians to Jews during the war. There were, of course, indigenous traditions of anti-Semitism, as well as a tendency to distinguish—as Prime Minister Rallis did—between "the Jews" of Salonika and the "Greek citizens of Jewish origin" in "Old Greece." Thus the authorities did not succeed in emulating the Danish Government's principled insistence to the Germans that all Danish Jews were regarded as full citizens. But they were clearly rather closer to this position than to that adopted by, say, the Vichy French or Slovak governments.

A further similarity with the Danish experience is the way a sort of spontaneous popular mobilization occurred against Nazi measures that stretched from the Athens police, the Church leadership to the resistance and ordinary farmers, peasants and townspeople. Perla Soussi, from Corfu, once told me about the Security Battalionist guarding her in Patras who had urged her to escape: she, however, refused to abandon her family.

Solomon Holho, from Salonika, hid out for many months on the island of Skopelos. The islanders, he told me, had so little idea of what a Jew was that they asked him one day: "You Jews, how do you make the sign of the cross?" And finally, there is the testimony of Alfredos Cohen, a lawyer from Athens, who recorded the spontaneous support of neighbors and friends in late 1943:

> I will never forget the terror which seized us one night while I was hiding my large family in one of the houses, when it was announced that the Germans had published an order declaring that all the Jews who

were caught in hiding would be shot, and the people who were hiding them would be sent to the concentration camp.

Then one of us said that it was not right for us to stay in that house and endanger the lives and peace of aged people and even women. The answer was: "No, you must stay. Indeed, my son, why should our lives be more precious than yours?"

In his introduction to October 1943, an account of the rescue of Danish Jewry, the Yiddish writer Sholem Asch insisted that "it is of the highest importance not only to record and recount, both for ourselves and for the future, the evidence of human degradation, but side by side with them to set forth the evidence of human exaltation and of nobility." This seems to me a useful guide to approaching the story of the Final Solution in Greece. To be sure, there is ample evidence of human degradation; but we will also find examples of altruism and courage.

We are still only at the beginning of this work and time is not on our side: of the approximately 10,000 Greek Jews who survived the war there are many elderly survivors whose stories should be recorded; there are also many non-Jewish Greeks, like those 161 individuals so far honored by the Israeli Government, whose testimonies must be preserved.

Finally, there are some valuable documentary collections inside Greece—stored at present in office basements, in safes, or cupboards—which stand in urgent need of preservation, cataloguing and microfilming. These sources collectively shed light not only on the events of the war years themselves, but on the period that followed too.

Contrary to Hitler's wishes, Jewish history did not end in the war. A research effort that is powerful enough to extend its range to our own times will enrich both our knowledge of the history of the Jews and—just as importantly—the history of Greece in all its aspects as well.

NOTES

1. PAAA, R 100870 ["Judenfrage in Griechenland, 1941–1943"], Suhr [RSHA]-Rademacher [AA], Berlin, July 11, 1942.

2. PAAA, *Deutsche Gesandtschaft* (Athens), vol. 66.

3. E. Counio-Amarilio, *Peninta chronia meta: anamniseis mais salonikiotissas evraias* (Salonika, 1995), p. 53.

4. N. Kokantzis, *Gioconda* (Salonika, 1975).

5. PAAA, vol. 69, Rallis-Altenburg, Oct. 7, 1943.

6. Yad Vashem archives, YV/M 4–5, Rescue Committee of the Jewish Agency
   for Palestine, Bulletin [Jan.–June 1945].

GREECE AND THE GREEK DIASPORA:
THE GREEK–AMERICAN COMMUNITY AT THE DAWN OF THE TWENTY-FIRST CENTURY, AND THE TWILIGHT OF THE TWENTIETH

John A. Koumoulides

"BIOGRAPHY is history and history is biography," observed the late Sir Ronald Syme, Camden Professor of Ancient History at the University of Oxford. This essay reflects personal experiences and observations of Hellenism in the United States of America during my 41-year-long life in America as a student and teacher. They are perspectives of a distant observer, and not of an "active" member of the Greek-American community. This paper is only an outline viewed from my own prism of the history of the Greek-American community, and I hope that it will be accepted as such. Before proceeding with this paper, however, I shall venture to share with the wider public what being a Hellene means to me.

During my lifetime I have been a product and a student of Greece and of Europe. In my early years in the land of my birth, the land that nurtured me, being Greek had not entered my consciousness the way it has during my years abroad. Actually, I do not recall the matter ever entering my thoughts and concerns. I was one of approximately ten million Greeks in the land of Greece, one whose parents experienced the trials of being *prosfiges*, refugees, and the trauma of having to leave, alas by force, the lands of their ancestors and birth. I am the child of *prosfiges*.

My mother and her parents were refugees from Argyroupolis of Trabezond, Pontos. My father, who was born in the Russian port city of Novorossisk of a Russian father and Greek mother, was orphaned at the age of two. His father, a prominent merchant and landowner, and loyal member of the Orthodox church, was murdered by the Bolsheviks for his support of the Tsar and the Church. In my own life I had first-hand knowledge of being a child of refugees, but not the melancholy experience. Actually, it was only when circumstances brought me to the shores of the United States of America in July of 1956, shortly after graduation from the

Gymnasium, that my ethnic and religious identity began to slowly but steadily enter my conscience.

Hellenes are the custodians of a great heritage. Being Greek means the privilege of being a member of a unique ethnic culture and reveling in its glorious history and humor, its language and literature, its music and idiosyncrasies and its festivals, and in general its contributions to the cultural identity of our Western civilization. Being a member of the Orthodox Church means being entrusted with the heritage of a great faith, a faith rich in rituals and ceremonies, tolerant and yet demanding, a loving and a caring faith, an ancient Christian faith that for centuries helped to nurture Hellenism. There is an indispensable link between Hellenism and Orthodoxy.

Being a Hellene in the United States of America means feeling a special love and affection for this land I have chosen as my second country, a land where love of freedom is as treasured as in the land where the idea of freedom was born and democracy was first practiced 2,500 years ago—in Athens, Greece. America has provided freedom and opportunity to millions from all parts of the world who have come and settled here. My parents raised me to believe in and be proud of my ethnic and religious heritage. Faith in God was my parents' treasure. Orthodoxy was its nourishment.

In the United States of America, a land of immigrants, I developed a strong consciousness of my Hellenic and Orthodox identity. I did not have to mute my ethnic and religious identity in order to be a "good American" for, on the contrary, America invites all its people to be what they are and to believe what they wish without fear. Indeed, it is from individual diversity and shared faith in God that Americans draw their strength and hope. The ethnic, racial, linguistic and religious mosaic of the United States is a microcosm of the cosmos. Orthodoxy and Hellenism are only two rather small stones of the American mosaic.

✺ ✺

The history of the Greeks in America can be divided into three periods. The first period starts with the sixteenth century and ends with the nineteenth century. The second covers the first half of our century. The third refers to the last 30 years, i.e., from 1960 to today.

It is alleged that the first Greeks to set foot on the New World were sailors. They were working on ships owned by the king of Spain, right after Christoforos Colombos, when the kingdom of Seville was at the first stage of expanding its dominance and trade to the new continent. The first historical mention of the Greeks is made by F. D. Bandelier, who states that in 1528 a Greek sailor, Don Theodoro or Theodoros, fell victim to the Indians in Florida.

Much later, in the eighteenth century, and more specifically in 1768, Greeks from Peloponnisos, especially from Mani, along with some Greeks from Asia Minor, arrived in Florida and settled in an area they called the colony of New Smyrna, Florida. Ten years later, as historian E. P. Panagopoulos states, they resettled a few miles to the north, in what is today St. Augustine, Florida. In 1864 the first Greek Orthodox Church in America was established in New Orleans, Louisiana.

The first American reference to Greeks dates from 1824 when, according to official documents, five immigrants arrived from Greece. According to one historical source, these were Greek orphans who seem to have been adopted by American philhellenes who participated in the struggle for the liberation of Greece (1821–29).

For the period between 1824 and the end of the century, we do not have any reliable data, official or unofficial. The year 1890, however, marks the start of the first great wave of immigration from areas of the Peloponnisos, as well as from the Asia Minor coast, mainly to the eastern coast of the United States. It is estimated that by the mid-1920s, 450,000 Greeks had emigrated to the United States. This number also includes refugees from Asia Minor and the Pontus region, although they did not constitute the majority in that period.[1]

The Greeks came to the New World mainly to better their economic condition. They were young men, sometimes children, who wanted to work, to save money, and to return to Greece to their villages and families. The ties with the fatherland remained strong. It is worth noting that 45,000 men of draft age, and along with them women and children, returned to their native land at the start of the Balkan Wars (1912–13) to enlist, as volunteers, in the Greek army. Another impressive characteristic is the amount of money sent to Greece. Official data for the period of 1910–30 show that more than 650 million dollars flowed into the country and strengthened the Greek economy. If one converts the value of the dollars of that period into their current value, one then gets a better picture of this truly important contribution by immigrants to the Greek economy.

Around 45 percent, i.e., more than 200,000 of the 450,000 immigrants of the 1890–1930 period, returned to Greece for permanent repatriation. Generally, we could say that there was no intention at that time of a permanent settlement in the United States. In other words, a great percentage of those young immigrants, by today's standards, could be considered "travellers."

The only difference was that their trip was a long one—it could sometimes last twenty or even thirty years. And certainly it was not at all a tourist trip. It was characterized by hard work, often wretched living conditions, and especially by the lack of feeling that they "belonged," that they were citizens with equal rights in their new country.

The second significant immigration period is the one between 1947 and 1960, when around 75,000 Greeks came to the United States of America. The third and last period (from 1960 to today) is characterized by the change in the immigration law in 1966, when with the active contribution of the first native-born member of Congress of Greek origin, Dr. John Brademas, Greek immigration to the United States was facilitated. From that time until 1980 about 160,000 people left Greece with the intention of settling permanently in the United States. However, during the 1980s their number was greatly reduced, falling to 25,000. Today the new immigrants number fewer than 1,000 per year.

Slowly but steadily, the Greek who has left his country during the twentieth century, looking for a better future in the United States, has acquired economic independence. Along with this independence has come social recognition, first within his own group and then within the wider American social and economic context. His children have been raised in a new environment, with new customs and ideas. A new social conscience has been formed within him. He is faced with dilemmas, created by everyday life, which cut across his familiar, religious and national beliefs. The Greek of America is constantly trying in every way to balance within himself the old values with the new. In an environment filled with political, minority, and psychological stress, he brings with him the heavy burden of a priceless heritage and of a long tradition, but he also has to face a new reality in his family and especially in his work and social environment that he cannot ignore.

Between the second and third period, a significant change took place in the character of the immigrants. The intent to return to the old country slowly diminished and in the end was extinguished, the only exception being its survival in some small pockets, mainly around New York and Chicago areas. The new immigrants consider America as their own country now. They get married, many times with non-Greeks and sometimes with non-Orthodox. They have decided to make their family and work in America. In short, their roots are on the other side now. It is worth noting that mixed marriages today constitute more than half of all marriages performed, and this is especially true for the western, mid-western, and southern states.

When Constantine Cavafy set to poetry the yearning of return, the Nostos of the Greek immigrant, he wrote:

Μέχρι γήρατος κατεκόπισα,
εἰργάσθην ἀπνευστὶ φωνῆς Ἑλλάδος
στερηθεὶς καὶ τῶν ὀχθῶν μακρὰν τῆς Σάμου.
Ὅθεν νῦν οὐδὲν
φριωτὸν πάσχ᾽ κ᾽ εἰς ἄδην δὲν πορεύομαι πενθῶν.
Ἐκεῖ θὰ εἶμαι μετὰ τῶν συμπολιτῶν.
Καὶ τοῦ λοιποῦ θὰ ὁμιλῶ ἑλληνιστί.

I toiled till my old age. I worked without a break
deprived of the sound of the Greek language
and the shores of distant Samos. Thus now nothing
horrible I suffer, nor do I go to Hades mourning. For there
I will be among my fellow countrymen;
and I'll always be speaking Greek.

Cavafy was primarily referring to and speaking about the Greeks of the first and, to some extent, the second immigration periods, those people we today call first- and second-generation Americans. Today and especially since the 1950s the Greek in the United States essentially lives in an environment virtually cut off from Greece. He functions, both he and his children, as Greek only in relation to the positive memories of the country of his parents and grandparents and the pride that he belongs to the Hellenes, a race with a history and glorious past that is greatly valued in his new country. Those memories and the pride, together with his faith in Orthodoxy, compose a deciding template of his Greekness.

Until the middle of the twentieth century, maybe until the 1960s, it was indeed correct for someone to call the Greeks of America "Greek Americans," since there was a living and functioning bond with Greece. Today, with the exception of the New York and Chicago pockets and the grandparents who are still alive from the second generation, it is more correct to speak about Americans of Greek descent. Here I would like to point out that this change does not mean that the Greek minority in the United States is losing its cohesion or its importance for the mother country. It simply means that the links in the chain that connects the two branches of the same tree are acquiring a different quality and different sensitivities.

> I love the church: its lavara, its silver vessels, its candleholders, the lights, the icons, the pulpit. Whenever I go there, into a church of the Greeks, with its aroma of incense, its liturgical chanting and harmony, the majestic presence of the priests, dazzling in their ornate vestments, the solemn rhythm of their gestures—my thoughts turn to the great glories of our race, to the splendor of our Byzantine heritage.[2]

"The Church is an earthly Heaven in which the super-celestial God dwells and walks about." Saint Germanos of Constantinople observes, "It represents the crucifixion, burial, and Resurrection of Christ. It is pre-figured in the patriarchs, foretold by the prophets, founded in the Apostles, adorned by the hierarchs, and fulfilled in the martyrs." Saint John of Kronstadt reminds us that, "In the Church are found all our blessings, our hopes and expectations, our peace, our joy; together with cleansing and sanctification. It is there that the truth of the future resurrection, of the victory over death, is often announced." The heritage of the Orthodox Church is an undivided part of the heritage of Hellenism. The Greek of today is the custodian of that extraordinary heritage, Orthodoxy and Hellenism.

The Church is the most important link between Orthodoxy and Hellenism. It is the guardian of the national conscience. Moreover, recognition by the church community is the first step to a wider social advancement. The common faith is what makes the Greek of the diaspora realize and maintain his ethnic identity and tradition. Through the awe-inspiring Byzantine teleturgical aspects of the Orthodox faith, the diaspora Greek is spiritually connected with the motherland, and accepts and is proud of his national heritage. Sir Steven Runciman very aptly remarked that, "Hellenism is nourished by Orthodoxy and Orthodoxy by Hellenism. They are indispensable to each other."[3]

The present situation in North America is the best example of the accuracy of the statement of the distinguished Scottish historian. Hier-

archs of the stature of the great Archbishop and later Patriarch Athina-
goras left their indelible presence.

The state of the Orthodox Church in the United States in the nineteenth century and early twentieth century was far from its present condition. The first priests in America had very little education. They faced
the same problems of language and social recognition as the rest of the
Greeks.[4] They were poor, and poor was their church. Their role and
contribution, however, were very significant. They became the link
among the first immigrants and the bridge that spiritually and mentally
connected them with the faith of their ancestors, their tradition, and
their fatherland.[5]

The Church held the Greeks together and forestalled their disappear-
ance within the great national and religious melting pot of America. In
1922 the Greek Orthodox Archdiocese of North and South America, under
the aegis of the Ecumenical Patriarchate, was established in New York.

Although to this day Orthodoxy and Hellenism continue to be synon-
ymous, at least within the wider masses of the faithful, during the last
decade impending changes have been noticeable. At the beginning of the
century, all the clergymen were born in Greece. Today 90 percent of all
priests who officiate in Greek Orthodox churches are born in America.
Most of them are graduates of the Holy Cross Greek Orthodox School of
Theology in Boston, and their mother tongue is English. For example, in
1968 the priest of the Holy Trinity Greek Orthodox Church in Indianap-
olis, Indiana, was born in Greece, the majority of the congregation were
born in Greece, and the liturgy was totally in Greek. Today the priest is
born in America of Greek parents, the congregation is only about 60
percent of Greek ancestry, and the liturgy is almost totally in English.
Such changes within the community, both in the composition of the
flock as well as in the language of liturgy, have taken place not only in
Indiana but also in most of the other states, with the possible exceptions
of New York and Chicago.

Here I should mention that most of the graduates of Holy Cross, and
especially those who aspire to climb the higher ecclesiastical echelons,
still consider it their obligation to spend at least one or more years at the
theological school of the University of Athens or of the University of
Thessaloniki. A comforting element that is attributed more, I would say,
to their personal initiative rather than an organized effort from this side
of the Atlantic—and something that should very seriously trouble us.

Another thing that should also trouble us is the wide lack of candidates for the rites of clergyman, which unfortunately does not replace—although it could very easily—from immigration.

In conclusion, we can maintain that the Church in America today is on the threshold of change from a pure "minority" with strong ties to the land of birth of the majority of the flock, to an American decree, fully adopted to the local conditions. At this crucial point, the preservation of Hellenism, as described above, is of immense importance. It requires correct strategy and careful handling, mainly because it refers to future generations where the bond with Greece weakens. For Orthodoxy to continue to comprise the source of Hellenism, it should adjust—at least some of its expression—following the passage of generations. The official statistics of the 1990 census show that 1,100,000 Americans declare they are of Greek descent. Of this number only 189,267 were born in Greece. Thus, based on this census, Greeks constitute only one half of one percent (0.5%) of the total population of the United States, approximately 270 million. It is of interest to note here that in most of the 435 Congressional districts, Greek Americans represent less than one percent of the registered voters. Naturally, the above numbers are conservative estimates and do not reflect the true power—and certainly not the dynamic presence—of the community.

But the figures that give us the number of Americans of Greek descent and of Americans born in Greece also show us a specific difference. These people statistically possess the highest degree of academic achievement, i.e., education and degrees, of any ethnic group in the United States. We may be short in numbers, but we are strong in education and in our power to influence the shaping of American policy.

The development of the second element, that of influence in the shaping of foreign policy toward Greece and Greek affairs, is rather recent. A significant role in this respect has been and is still being played by a small number of Americans of Greek descent who distinguished themselves in politics and became widely known.

The developments following the Cyprus tragedy in the summer of 1974 speak for themselves. A handful of gifted politicians, with the significant and always indispensable assistance and support of Philhellenes in Congress and the universities, were able not only to affect positively the shaping of American foreign policy toward Greece and Cyprus, but in some cases even to dictate it.

These people hold a respectable position within American society and have a dynamic presence. They command general respect and are known for their patriotism and honesty. Politicians with excellent education at the best universities of the United States and England have reached high positions from New York to California and are bringing honor everywhere to the Greek name.

The struggles in Congress of former Representative John Brademas, Senator Paul Sarbanes, and Senator Olympia J. Snowe, many other American politicians of Greek descent, such as the late Senator Paul Tsongas and former Representatives Nick Galifianakis, Gus Yatron, Peter Kyros, and Skip Bakalis; and later Representatives Michael Bilirakis, George W. Gekas, Ron Klink, and Nick Pappas; and Peter Maroudas, Chief of Staff to U.S. Senator Paul Sarbanes, have been amply documented. At the state and local level other politicians, such as the former governor of Massachusetts, Michael Dukakis, and many state representatives and senators, mayors, and other officials from both American political parties, in conjunction with Greek Americans from the world of business and academia, have played and still play an important role in the evolution of events. Various organizations that in the past were associated only with local affairs were soon transformed into Greek lobbies and became the pillars of Greek and Cyprus advocacy.

I have mentioned Philhellenes in the Congress. One who is especially distinguished is the former chairman of the Foreign Relations Committed of the U.S. House of Representatives, Lee H. Hamilton of Indiana. Representative Benjamin A. Gilman of New York and many others in both the Senate and the House of Representatives with their concern and support of issues on Greece and Cyprus have had a positive influence in the shaping of American policy towards Greece and Cyprus.

An important role in the shaping of public opinion as well as in the formation and continued existence of the lobbies has been and continues to be played by the Greek-American press. Newspapers like the *National Herald* and *Proini* in New York, the *Hellenic Chronicle* in Boston, and other Greek- and English-language papers in Chicago and California, along with the Orthodox *Observer* of the Greek Orthodox Church in America, as well as periodicals and other publications form a living mosaic that presents, represents, and unites all the smaller groups of the community. Many radio programs broadcasting in the Greek language operate in large cities. There is also information originating from Greek radio and television stations, especially in New York and Chicago.

Both the newspapers and radio stations receive most of their programs and material from stations and newspapers in Greece and Cyprus. In general terms the press, radio, and TV serve as a link between the United States and Greece and Cyprus.

The Americans believe that their civilization has its roots in and is a successor mainly to three older civilizations, all of which evolved around the Mediterranean, i.e., those of Israel, Greece, and Rome. From the Hebrews Americans took their Judeo-Christian foundation, from the Romans their political system, and from the Greeks the ideals of freedom and democracy.[6]

Philhellenism, in its wider context, became a strong propulsive force for the nascent American nation. The admiration of the fathers of the American democracy for the ancient Greeks and their civilization is well known. As an example, the Federalist Papers reveal that the Founding Fathers were well read in the classics and some of them knew Greek and Latin. Plato and Aristotle, Herodotus and Thucydides, Polybios and Plutarch, Sallust and Livy, Cicero and Tacitus served as sources for the drawing of parallels and lessons.

Greek and Latin were systematically taught in the nine Colonial Colleges, from Harvard, Dartmouth, Brown, and Yale in the north, to King's College (Columbia), Queen's College (Rutgers), College of New Jersey (Princeton), and the University of Pennsylvania in the center, to William and Mary in the south. For some thirty years in particular, between 1760 and 1790, the Greek and Latin classics enjoyed a great popularity in the thirteen states. Writing in 1765, the Bostonian John Adams advised: "Let us study...the history of the ancient ages; contemplate the great examples of Greece and Rome...."[7] For Adams "the republics of Greece and Rome were the seats of liberty." In a letter to Lafayette, he adds:

> Two republican powers, Athens and Rome, have done more honor to our species (humanity) than all the rest of it. A new country can be planted only by such government.[8]

The best illustration of Philhellenism among the Founding Fathers is Thomas Jefferson, the writer of the Declaration of Independence, George Washington's Secretary of State, and third President of the United States (1801–1809). His writings and his policies reveal that he was an enthusiastic Philhellene—a student, admirer, and lover of Hellenism.[9]

Philhellenism is still a huge force for Greece. We should not forget that while the Greeks of America are Greeks by origin, the philhellenes are Greeks by choice. The American scholars, "those partaking of our own education," know and admire Hellenism, mostly through the works of philhellenes. They know Edith Hamilton's *The Greek Way*, about ancient Greece; Sir Steven Runciman's *Byzantine Style and Civilization*, about Byzantine civilization; *Modern Greece*, by Charles Crawley, about modern Greece; and *The Orthodox Way*, by Bishop Kallistos of Diockleia, about Orthodoxy.

American young people are in touch with the history of Greece from their early school years through their college years. It would not be an exaggeration if I stated that the average American knows more about Greece than the average Greek knows about America.

In fact, the average American youth might know more about ancient Greek civilization than about the modern history of his own country.

These roots give us an encouraging picture of the future of Greek studies and through them the maintenance of the ties between modern Greece and the United States. Here I must stress, however, that this is more true of ancient Greek history, less true of Byzantine civilization, and much less, if at all, true of modern Greek history. It is true that the tragedy of Cyprus became the spark and the impetus for the creation of centers for modern Greek studies, but I am afraid that these centers today exist more in name than in essence. With the exception of New York and California, the spreading of modern Greek civilization is limited to the heroic efforts of a small number of Greek-American academics and the support of a larger number of Philhellenes. An example is my own university, Ball State, in Muncie, where only two Greek families reside. The program of Greek studies that had operated there since 1969 has managed to attract the most eminent authorities on Greek matters, through conferences and lectures on ancient, Byzantine, and modern Greek history, as well as on the civilization and history of Cyprus. An effort that can also yield fruit is the encouragement offered to young Americans to spend a summer in Greece. During the last 20 years, 50 students from my university have visited Greece and studied its civilization.

These efforts, this "proselytizing" of young Americans with respect to modern Greece, fortunately extend to other states besides Indiana and New York. It is one of the best ways to cross-fertilize the two countries in the future.

As I mentioned earlier, at the turn of the century most of the Greeks in America had their roots in Greece. Today the opposite is true. The majority of them are Americans of Greek descent with their roots and future in America. The bonds and memories that connected them with Greece in 1900 are quite different from those of 1997. Perhaps as a barometer for this development we could use the number of Social Security checks that the American embassy in Athens distributes to those who return to reside permanently in Greece; this number has declined greatly since 1960. There has also been a significant reduction in the amount of money sent to relatives in Greece, a poor country with rich citizens, as many in America believe today. The big boat trips of the 1950s with the full trunks, the gifts, and the dazzling American cars running through the narrow streets of Greek villages belong to history.

The belfries, the schools, the hospitals, and the foundations, along with donations to villages of origin, have been also reduced with the passing of time. Today the parents and uncles and most of the closest family members of Americans of Greek descent live and flourish within the geographical boundaries of the United States. English is the language of the parents and their children and Greek Orthodox their religion.[10]

These are the changes, of which I hope we are all aware. I hope they will become the compass for the shaping of the right policy, Greek and American, as far as the community is concerned.

In conclusion, please allow me to offer, based on my personal experience, some exhortations:

First, we must at any cost avoid the politicization of the community. The credo of the diaspora Greek in America is and must always be that he/she is an American proud and respectful of his/her Hellenic descent and Orthodox faith.

Second, as my good friend, the senior United States Senator from Maryland Senator Paul Sarbanes, has repeatedly stated, "We Greeks must be and remain united." Through unity, self-respect, and great solidarity we will be able further to enhance the power of Hellenism in this great country that has become our second motherland.

Third, during these last years the community and its leaders were undoubtedly able to help Greece in such matters as the struggle to keep the 7-to-10 ratio, and on the Skopje and the Cyprus issue. It must not, however, escape our attention that, since with the passing of time the new generations will have fewer common interests with Greece, the solid and steady basis for the preservation of the ties between Greece and the community cannot be anything else than our common cultural and religious origins and heritage.

Our efforts should lay the foundations for a continuous struggle to keep the Greek diaspora in the New World firmly and fully a part of the body of Hellenism and Orthodoxy. Let us live up to the heritage of our past and the promise of a bright future. Indeed, let us work for a Greece that it is proud of its past, but not live in it.

The Greeks of America are an incalculable force. They are a community full of vim and vigor that struggles for peace and justice and strongly defends the rights of Greece and Cyprus.

I am full of hope for tomorrow. But it will require struggle on both sides of the Atlantic, struggle that is so necessary for the realization of what my good friend the late President of the Republic of Greece, Constantinos Tsatsos, so eloquently wrote in 1978: "All of us together, with God's help should fulfill our duty, as human beings and Greeks, and leave as our bequest to our children and grandchildren our glorious inheritance...and not forget the holy ground where our seeds are found; small in area but great in glory, our first motherland."

> *Nescio qua natale solum dulcedine captos,*
> *Ducit, et immemores non sinit esse sui.*

> By some strange charm, our native land doth hold us captive
> nor permits that we should ever forget her.

> Ovid, *Epistolae ex Ponto*

NOTES

1. On the Greeks of Asia Minor and Trapezond, see the excellent study of Neal Aschenson, *Black Sea* (London: Jonathan Cape, 1995).

2. George Savidis (ed.), *C.P. Cavafy: Collected Poems* (Princeton: Princeton University Press, 1984), p. 44.

3. Steven Runciman, Sir, *The Great Church in Captivity* (Cambridge: Cambridge University Press, 1968), p. viii.

4. See James S. Scofield, "Forgotten History: The Klan vs Americans of Hellenic Heritage," *The Greek American* (August 9, 1997) 7.

5. See Charles C. Moskos, *Greek Americans. Struggle and Success* (New Brunswick: Transaction Publishers, 1989), p. 2.

6. See John A. Koumoulides (ed.), *The Good Idea. Democracy in Ancient Greece* (New York: Aristide D. Caratzas, 1995).

7. See Demetrios J. Constantelos, "Thomas Jefferson and His Philhellenism" *Journal of Modern Hellenism*, 12-13 (Winter 1995-96) 155-73.

8. *Ibid*.

9. See also, Carl J. Richards, *The Founders and the Classics—Greece, Rome and the American Enlightenment* (Cambridge: Harvard University Press, 1994).

10. According to the Statistical Charter of the Greek Orthodox Archdiocese of North and South America, between 1976 and 1992 there were 149,224 baptisms and 89,560 marriages, of which 35,767 were between Orthodox and 63,790 inter-Christian. For the same 16-year period, there were 6,629 divorces between Orthodox and 5,532 between inter-Christian couples. There were also 61,964 deaths and 13,490 Christians registered. For the Midwest region for the period 1 January 1992 to 31 December 1992, the diocese of Chicago registered 714 baptisms and 678 weddings, of which 244 were Orthodox and 434 mixed. The diocese of Detroit registered 494 baptisms and 310 weddings, of which 74 were Orthodox and 226 mixed. The diocese of Denver registered 412 baptisms and 206 weddings, of which 49 were Orthodox and 17 mixed. *Greek Orthodox Church of North and South America, Yearbook 1994* (New York: Greek Orthodox Archdiocese of North and South America), pp. 94-96. See also, Stephen J. Dubner, "Choosing My Religion," *The New York Times Magazine* (March 31, 1996), pp. 86-41 and b76.

CONTRIBUTORS

JOSEPH GILL, S.J., was Tutor in Medieval History at Campion Hall, the University of Oxford. His numerous publications include, *The Council of Florence, Personalities in the Council of Florence*, and *Byzantium and the Papacy 1198–1400*.

JASPER GRIFFIN is Professor of Classical Literature and Public Orator at the University of Oxford, where he is a fellow of Ballio College. His books include *Homer on Life and Death* and *Latin Poets and Roman Life*.

DAVID HUNT, Sir, was a fellow of Magdalen College, the University of Oxford, and an archaeologist before 1939. After war service with the army he entered the Diplomatic service in 1947; he was Private Secretary to Attlee and Churchill as Prime Ministers and subsequently High Commissioner in Uganda, Cyprus, and Nigeria and Ambassador to Brazil. In addition to other books, he has edited and contributed to *Footprints in Cyprus*.

BERNARD M.W. KNOX is Director Emeritus of Harvard's Center for Hellenic Studies in Washington, D.C. His essays and reviews have appeared in numerous publications. His works include *The Oldest Dead White European Males and Other Reflections on Classics; Backing into the Future: The Classical Tradition and Its Renewal*. He is the editor of *The Norton Book of Classical Literature*.

JOHN A. KOUMOULIDES is Professor of History at Ball State University in Muncie, Indiana. He has written and edited numerous books on Greece and Cyprus, his latest being *The Monastery of Tatarna: History and Treasures* (jointly with Lazaros Deriziotis and Stavroula Sdrolia) and *The Good Idea: Democracy in Ancient Greece*. He is Corresponding Member of the Academy of Athens.

173

MARY R. LEFKOWITZ is Andrew R. Mellon Professor in the Humanities at Wellesley College. Her publications include *Not Out of Africa: How Afrocentrism Became an Excuse to Teach Myth as History* and *Black Athena Revisited*.

MARK MAZOWER is Professor of History at the University of Sussex. His book *Inside Hitler's Greece: The Experience of Occupation 1941–1944* was joint winner of the 1993 Fraenkel Prize and the Longman's History Book of the Year prize.

DONALD M. NICOL is Koraes Professor Emeritus of Byzantine and Modern Greek Studies at King's College, University of London. His numerous publications include *The Last Centuries of Byzantium, 1261–1453*, *Church and Society in the Last Centuries of Byzantium* and *The End of the Byzantine Empire*.

EDWARD PECK, Sir, was educated at Clifton College (Bristol) and Queen's College, University of Oxford. He entered the Consular Service, spending time in Spain, Bulgaria, Turkey, and Greece. He served as Under Secretary of State for Defence and Related Matters. He was also British Permanent Representative to the North Atlantic Council.

RONALD SYME, Sir, was Camden Professor of Ancient History at the University of Oxford. His books include *The Roman Revolution*, *Tacitus*, *Colonial Elites*, *Emperors and Biography*, *The Historia Augusta*, and *Roman Papers*.

INDEX

A